The Golden Rules for a Happy Life

PHILIP HESKETH

Contents

CHAPTER 1

What Ifs, If Onlys, Maybes and the First Golden Rule

If you could use just one word from the English language to sum up life and business, then for me that word would have to be *unpredictable*. Naturally, life can be many other things too. Happy or sad, exhilarating or mundane, a breeze or a struggle. But the one thing you can be sure of is that things will happen when you least expect them. Plans will be dashed, rugs pulled from under our feet and doors slammed shut in our faces. Just like the man who told Queen that 'Bohemian Rhapsody' would never be a successful single, sometimes you just don't see it coming.

Your background too, is full of what ifs, if onlys and maybes.

But there are seven Golden Rules we can learn from history for you to be happier and more successful and make your life more predictable. And 50 other lessons about life, business and everything that can be learned from historical events.

Starting with the very early beginnings of the Wars of the Roses, this book has at its heart several key acts in English history that changed things for ever. And, more importantly, there are valuable lessons to be learned.

Because the key acts are all caused by people. And their decisions not only often made *them* unhappier and less successful, but many, many other people too. Learn those lessons yourself and live your life by the Golden Rules and you will be happier and more fulfilled.

The study of history has become less popular in schools over the past few years; the proportion of students taking history GCSE has steadily declined. When it is studied, it seems to me that subjects and periods are examined in isolation, without being related to the march of events and their meaning – either then or now.

It strikes me that history is sometimes seen in schools as an intellectual indulgence, without practical application. And yet studying what has happened in the past helps us not to make the same mistakes in the future.

And that's the real purpose of this book.

Ironically – and thankfully – there is great interest amongst adults in history and what we can learn from it. The 500th anniversary of Henry VIII's accession was almost treated as breaking news, with a flood of TV programmes, features and columns. Indeed, our daily news is saturated with history. The MPs' expenses scandal that happened at the same time as the accession anniversary can be appreciated only through the encrusted pattern of parliamentary priv-ilege and a culture of moat maintenance at public expense going back centuries. We, the great unwashed, seem to instinctively understand the importance of linking history with modern life. And this book is effectively about power, human interactions and the ramifications of actions taken for the wrong reasons.

And although its focus is very much on Henry VIII and his three offspring, who also ruled the country, it really starts with the Wars of the Roses.

To many people, the Wars of the Roses was simply a century-long feud between two rival counties in the north of England. Few are aware of the causes, fewer still the outcome. One or two of the battles may ring a bell and occa-sionally a place name may sound familiar. Like Pontefract or Eccles, or indeed anything associated with a snack or pastry. I'm told the Battle of Hobnob was a particularly bloody affair, but the details have largely been lost with the passage of time. What I'm really interested in – and what the focus of this book will be – are the lessons we could and should learn from a particularly hairy period of history from Henry VIII coming to the throne to the end of the reign of his daughter, Elizabeth I, some 70 years later.

However, the first key act I will briefly look at that changes English history is in 1377 when the king of England, Edward III, dies and his grandson, Richard, becomes king. He's only ten so it's decided that his uncle, the Duke of Lancaster, will run the country. It's the real start of the Wars of the Roses.

And arguably the biggest decision that changes things forever is in 1533 when Henry VIII – the son of the Lancastrian Henry VII who effectively ended the Wars of the Roses by taking a Yorkist wife – decides he will marry Anne Boleyn, having decided to get a divorce from Katherine of Aragon. And Henry changes not only the face of English history but sets in motion a chain of events that will see a remarkable number of people beheaded, hung, drawn and quartered, burned at the stake and imprisoned, and also will see his daughter, Elizabeth, die without issue and the uniting of the Scottish and English thrones for the first time.

Was Henry VIII a vain, self-pitying, arrogant, overweight bully with few scruples and even fewer morals, who was neither a marital nor a martial success?

Was he simply a lousy politician and a worse diplomat who made a prat of himself abroad?

Or was he our best-known king for good reason?

Well, Henry VIII seems to me to have been the sort of bloke who, if faced with a choice between having a lukewarm, milky drink and sticking his genitals in a hornets' nest, would inevitably head straight towards the sound of the buzzing whilst unbuckling his belt.

We English do seem to find something very appealing in the sense of daring and total commitment in the style of battle that is personified by such diverse figures as Horatio Nelson, Ian 'Beefy' Botham, 'Hurricane' Higgins, 'Captain Marvel' Bryan Robson and Ronnie 'The Rocket'

O'Sullivan. We took 'Freddie' Flintoff to our hearts not because he was the best wicket-taker or run-getter but, rather, because we could imagine him leaping between a ship's rigging, sword drawn, masts burning overhead and with blood and gore spattered all around him.

Similarly, the nation was bizarrely amused and impressed when Boris Johnson, waving a Union flag in each hand, rode down a zip line to promote the London Olympics in 2012 but was left dangling inelegantly in front of a watching crowd. The then Mayor of London spent around five minutes hanging comically from the drooping line wearing a hard hat, as spectators took video footage and photographs of his misfortune. When one asked how he was feeling, he replied, 'Very, very well thank you,' before shouting to bystanders, 'Get me a rope, get me a ladder.' 'It's very, very well organised,' he assured them. 'It's going well so far.'

The English have a weakness for clever buffoons and 'cards'. Boris's admirers rejoice in his indiscretions. Here at last, they say, is somebody real; a man who tells it like it is; an overweight bundle of fun who makes them laugh. And he became prime minister in 2019 despite his errors of judgement, mistakes and many calamitous gaffes that would have seen off many contenders for that post.

Like Freddie, Boris and Beefy, Henry is the sort of king – the sort of 'character' – you don't see very often nowadays.

Fact is, he was the pivot around which English history revolves, and there are things we should learn from Henry.

We then follow the reigns of Henry's son, then his eldest daughter – destined to have the sobriquet 'Bloody Mary' – and finally the reign of his third child – at least the third to reign – by which time the inventor of the bicycle, the potato and tobacco, Sir Walter Raleigh, as well as the bard himself, William Shakespeare, are all on the scene. Writing, peddling and chain smoking their way through the next few decades whilst still wondering whether to mash or fry those damn spuds.

So, as I say, the purpose of this book is not simply to recount the tale of the reign of Henry VIII and the reigns of his three children for their own sake. The story of arguably the two best-known monarchs we have ever had provides us with much more than just a fascinating insight into man's inhumanity to man throughout the Middle Ages.

It also tells us about every facet of mankind and provides us with uncanny parallels with modern life. This period is the beginning of religious life as we know it, and Henry's divorce is the end of the beginning.

I use this period of English history as a conduit to outline the lessons for life, business and everything. Every chapter in this book has at least one valuable lesson in either life or business.

And there are not one but seven Golden Rules.

Of course, it would be easy to say that with the benefit of hindsight we could all easily learn the lessons. So, I have endeavoured to avoid the 'smart after the event approach'. A very significant percentage of the failures and mistakes we have made make repeating patterns, and there are usually warning signs that, in retrospect, were obvious. I shall make more than just the odd passing reference to the British liner *Titanic*. It has become symbolic of things that go wrong. It is a classic example of warning signs that were all too clear well before it left Southampton in 1912. And the very fact that people were not willing to point out those kinds of warning signs is also looked at in depth.

People throughout history have appeared not to have learned the first Golden Rule. So, before we get into the heart of the book – here's the first Golden Rule for love, life, business and everything.

THE FIRST GOLDEN RULE:

WHEN YOU LOSE, DON'T LOSE THE LESSON.

History is usually written by the victors and so often the defeated are guilty of hubris and don't actually learn the lesson. Too often we lose in love and in life but don't look at how and why we lost.

And make changes.

The happy and successful people are those who analyse themselves harshly and learn the lesson before they move on. For sure, having run a business, I learned more from mistakes and making bad judgements than I did from doing the right things. Or, sometimes, just being lucky.

But before we get into the Wars of the Roses and then the Tudor period, allow me to transport you back in time to the summer of 1971 in Greater Manchester. I was standing outside the main hall in Ashton-under-Lyne Grammar School waiting for the invigilator to call us in to sit a physics A Level paper. Expectations were running high and confidence was flowing freely.

Earlier that term I had experienced a brief lunchtime meeting with the careers advisor. He was twice my age and sported long hair and a beard in the manner of a certain footballer at that time, George Best. Despite his tweed jacket, I felt I could trust him implicitly. Besides, he must have been good at his job because it took him only ten minutes to map out my entire future having learned just two things about me.

Firstly, that I was studying maths, further maths and physics, and secondly that I was in the Scouts and so liked the outdoor life. From this he expertly concluded that I should apply to Bath University to study civil engineering.

I was to be a civil engineer, carving up the countryside, sculpting the landscape, wallowing in mud. It would be my job, nay, my destiny, to construct bridges and build roads for the good people of Britain. All I had to do was pass the physics exam and my future was as good as sealed.

There was, however, one unforeseen problem on the horizon. And it came in the form of a woman. Well, almost a woman to be precise. You see, for the best part of the previous three years I had been completely and totally head over heels in love with a girl three years my junior.

Susan Garlick was unaware of my feelings for her. She barely knew I existed. But then, with me at the age of 18 and about to leave school for a richly rewarding life as a road builder, I realised that if I didn't act soon I would be carrying a heavy heart under my bright yellow jacket. Beneath my hard, protective helmet, my head would still be spinning for Susan. Nothing much would be happening to my feet but I would be wearing steel toe-capped boots just to be on the safe side. It's the law, apparently.

The problem was I didn't have the courage to ask her out myself. Instead, I persuaded one of my fellow physics students, Trevor 'Sid' Smith, to ask her for me. He was instructed to ascertain whether or not she would be willing to meet me alone outside school – and under no circumstances to embellish the offer with any fanciful notions that might lead to grass stains or other such unde-sirable marks on her school uniform. Sid could get carried away at times, but I was relying on him to be delicate and discreet. The problem was that despite weeks of prodding and encouraging him to do the deed, he chose the morning of the physics exam to actually approach her.

To make matters worse, Sid arrived at the hall at exactly the same time the exam hall doors were opened. I asked eagerly if he had spoken to her and he nodded. Just at this moment the invigilator ushered us into the hall and told us to remain silent until the end of the exam. I silently mouthed the word 'Well?' to Sid with my eyes widening manically to represent the question mark. But Sid remained silent. He even ignored my best Marcel Marceau impression for a quick thumbs up or down to signal Susan's answer.

And so that was it. My fate was sealed. I hardly wrote a thing, failed the physics A level exam, and never did get to Bath. I did a third year in the Sixth Form to make amends for my failure and, during this time, worked on the dustbins with Michael Bamforth who was reading psychology at York. He got me interested in the subject and I eventually went on to Newcastle University to study for a BSc in it.

And the rest, as they say, is history. But actually, it was also the beginning of a lifetime wondering what would have happened if Sid had not spoken to Susan Garlick on that particular day. If he had arrived at school either early enough to tell me her answer or too late for me to have questioned him at all. Perhaps I would have been in a different frame of mind, passed the exam and gone to Bath. Right now, I could be standing in a field somewhere, up to my knees in mud and gazing expertly through a theodolite.

I would never have gone to Newcastle and never have met and married my wife. I would be married to a completely different woman altogether.

What ifs and if onlys and maybes.

All our lives are full of them.

And there is something else too. Something that is fundamental to our feelings about happiness and success.

It is that thing we call 'hope'. You can lose it, have it dashed, or never be without it. Some say it springs eternal, others that it never dies. But what exactly is it? Modern dictionaries define hope as *'a feeling of desire for something and a confidence in the possibility of its fulfilment'*. The key word is 'possibility'. That's why every Saturday night millions of people sit with bated breath and fingers crossed hoping that they'll get lucky. And then there are those that do the lottery.

Hope can be a rejection of cynicism and defeatism. But every business, just like every individual, needs it. In their darkest days incarcerated in a Beirut bunker, Keenan, McCarthy and Waite never lost hope that one day they would be set free. Similarly, Liverpool fans knew in the summer of 1990 that at some time in the future they would once again win the top league championship in England. They didn't think at the time it would take 30 years, of course, but at least they weren't chained to a radiator in the meantime.

Hope has proven to be the key ingredient to create resilience in captives and survivors of traumas such as natural disasters. Studies show that people who score high on hope cope better with disease, illness and even pain. When relationships are at an all-time low, it's a fact that people get ill more often. Moreover, the presence of *contempt* in a marriage has such a negative effect on the immune system that it can influence how many *colds* a couple get.

A fact not to be sneezed at.

It's clear then that hope influences many aspects of our daily life and can shape our perception of reality. But, of course, as a reader of this book, what you are really interested in is how *you* can be happier and more successful by learning the lessons from the past. And I will reveal exactly that over the 18 chapters. But it all starts with daring to hope. So here's the first of our fifty lessons for life:

Never deprive someone of hope; it might be all they have.

All the decisions made by these historical figures were made because they hoped that things would be better by making those decisions. But they appear to have, in the most part, not to have learned the Golden Rules.

The Golden Rules that we all need to learn to live a happy and successful life keep coming up again and again.

Well, that's my story and I'm going to share it with you.

CHAPTER 2

The Build-Up to The Big Man, the Wars of the Roses and the Second Golden Rule

When Henry VIII came to the throne in 1509 he was, as we all are, the product of his upbringing. We all only have one childhood and it's not our fault. A subject we will return to as one of the Golden Rules.

Our parents in turn – their views, their attitudes and the way they see the world – are the product of *their* parents.

So to better understand the reign of Henry VIII, we really need to look back over the previous 150 years or so before he came to the throne, to help us comprehend his actions that have their repercussions even now. And, in particular, the battles for the English throne that are known as the Wars of the Roses.

In the middle of the 14th century the population of England was just over three million. It had been as high as six million but the Black Death had taken its toll. And, believe it or not, Calais was part of England then. The king at the time – Edward III – had believed himself to be the rightful king of France and had captured the city in 1347.

A battle that Henry VIII continued to fight in the 16th century.

Edward III's ten-year-old grandson Richard – a Yorkist like his father – was the next king but thought too young to rule, so his uncle, John of Gaunt, the Duke of Lancaster, effectively ran the country. The Lancastrian Gaunt wrestled control from the Yorkist king and, at an early stage, we see the impact of disunity, struggle for power and greed.

So often it is disunity and greed in personal and business relationships that makes things go wrong. A theme we shall return to several times in this book.

In 1383 Richard II celebrated reaching the ripe old age of 15 by marrying Anne of Bohemia but she died of the plague a few years later and, with them not having had children, a cunning plan was hatched for Richard to marry Isabella of France, then aged just seven. As plans go, it wasn't one of the best.

It wasn't until the child bride got off the ferry at Dover clutching a little teddy bear that Richard realised his error.

But, at the end of October 1396, King Richard married Isabella of France.

Yes, a nine-year-old French girl.

Perhaps there are some more obvious things we can learn from history. A marriage between a nine-year-old bride and a 29-year-old groom is likely to have problems. So it's no surprise this one didn't quite work out and Isabella later married her own cousin and died aged 19.

However, it was upon the death of John of Gaunt in 1399 that things really started to hot up. He'd all but ruled England for the previous 22 years so his son, Henry, now Duke of Lancaster, was expecting to take over the family firm. However, Richard, the Yorkist boy king, was now not only grown up and shaving but had already been twice married and, even more importantly, was still alive. So Henry had him incarcerated in Pontefract Castle. When he died the following year. Henry had his body put on public display in St Paul's Cathedral to show everyone he was very, very dead – aged 33. Henry of Lancaster became king.

He was to be king for just 14 years and have seven children. Upon his death in 1413 he was succeeded by Henry V.

And he inherited not only the throne but also his father's enemies.

Henry V was 27 when he proposed to marry Catherine of Valois. That's right, another French girl, demanding the old Plantagenet lands of Normandy and Anjou as his dowry. The French didn't think much of that so Henry declared war.

It really was that easy in those days.

Having won the Battle of Agincourt in 1415 the defeated French king accepted Henry V as heir to the French crown. Had Henry lived a mere two months longer, he would have been king of both England and France but he died in France in 1422. His wife Catherine had borne his only son the year before while he was away, and Henry never saw his son and heir, Henry VI.

Was it all worth it? He spent so much time at work he died of exhaustion and didn't get to have time with his young son. Never held his hand on that walk on the first day at infants school. Never saw him appear in a nativity play nor taught him how to swim or ride a bike.

As so many men find when they spend too much time at work and not enough time on the really important issues such as simply spending time with your children, the regret comes later. Or as Joni Mitchell once famously said, 'You don't know what you've got 'til it's gone.'

It's a lesson we should all heed.

Your children only get one childhood.

So if you are a parent, set yourself the goal of attending *all* your children's athletics contests, plays, performances and 'meet-the-teacher' evenings. Teach them to ride a bicycle, to throw a ball, to develop a signature, to cook, to bake, to fly a kite; teach them that you will always be there for them.

Obviously, Henry VI was only a few months old when he became king so his father's brothers ran the shop for him. Sound familiar?

When he finally came of age he proudly maintained the family tradition of marrying a niece of the French king, Margaret of Anjou.

The reign of Henry VI is arguably the most calamitous in the whole of English history. At the start of his reign he was king of all England and France because of all the warmongering and conquering of his father. Thirty years later all that was left other than his homeland was Calais. A little bit of France left for us.

The Lancastrian Henry VI had married Queen Margaret when she was 16 and she gave birth to a son, Edward, in 1453. And that meant the 31-year-old Richard, Duke of York, needed to advance his claims on the throne of England and, at the same time, settle a score with the Lancastrians. And so, on May 22nd 1455 the first battle of the Wars of the Roses took place in St Albans.

That's right; we've got there at last.

The Yorkists defeated the king's army and the Lancastrian King Henry VI was taken prisoner. During captivity he suffered what was referred to as 'bouts of insanity' so Richard, Duke of York, was made Protector of England.

The White Rose fans were singing and dancing in the streets. Except there were no streets in 1455; just sort of dust tracks through villages, but you get the idea. However, their happiness was short lived. Because less than a year later, the king was declared perfectly sane. He immediately retook the throne of England and Lancashire once again ruled.

Needless to say, only four years later the Yorkists and Lancastrians were spoiling for another fight to decide who ruled England.

The Yorkists won the next battle and also captured King Henry VI for a *second* time. Despite the King being incarcerated, his wife, Queen Margaret of Anjou, was still on the loose. Worse still, she was even more frightening than the King.

Seething mad and spitting feathers, she headed straight for Yorkshire having raised an army of Lancastrians. She's in a bit of a state. You can be in *the* right state and you can be in *a* right state and, at the time, she favoured the latter.

Next lesson in life; if you are getting ready for a fight, be in the right state and not in a right state.

And so, in December 1460, the duke's 4,000 men took on the Queen's 20,000-strong army of Lancastrians at the Battle of Wakefield. Richard's men were 'environed on every side, like fish in a net' according to an eyewitness who had obviously been drinking. The appeal for a mismatch was overruled. Both Richard, Duke of York, and his 18-year-old son, Edmund died in the battle and

Queen Margaret had their severed heads displayed on Micklegate Bar in York. The Lancastrians' advantage was restored.

It's at this point that the Wars of the Roses gets a trifle confusing if you always thought it was simply a series of battles between two counties in the north of England and two great-grandsons of Edward III.

In the red corner we have the Lancastrians (based in Yorkshire) aided by an assortment of Welsh and Scottish mercenaries. Whilst in the white corner we have the Yorkists, made up mainly of southerners based in Shropshire.

Desperate to avenge the previous year's defeat on home soil, the Yorkists, now led by Edward, the son of Queen Margaret and Henry VI, fought like tigers in the battle of Towton.

On Palm Sunday in March 1461, just as the rest of the country were tucking into their Easter eggs and checking out the Bank Holiday sport, the rivers around Towton ran red with Lancastrian blood. The Yorkists were victorious and Edward IV was crowned king – the first Yorkist king. And for what?

The crown?

What we see in the Wars of the Roses are fights for territory and power – still the most common cause of modern-day conflict today.

Nowadays it's as global as nations fighting and as local as road rage, trolley rage and gangs from postcodes scrapping for territory.

Back then, the top echelons of society were developing and, with it, the habit of fighting under leaders; first selected for ability and suitability, then selected for life, and finally born to the job. Imagine the shiver sent down the spine of a young, peace-loving heir to the throne on the realisation that one day they may have to lead the troops into battle.

You'd pretty soon be devising a strategy that saw you leading from the rear. Or possibly even an armchair back in the palace.

But this is the background to Henry VIII. His whole family history is about the search for power and domination.

And Henry VI? Well, eventually the Yorkists caught up with him.

Deposed, depressed – and in deep doo-doo, after his capture he was incarcerated for a *third* time and put in the Tower of London.

Peace then returned to the country as the Yorkist King Edward IV consolidated his reign, formed a stable government, either sacked or conciliated the Lancastrian supporters and married a beautiful Lancastrian widow, Elizabeth Wydville in 1464.

And Elizabeth provided Edward with an heir, Edward, and a spare, Richard (later to be the Princes in the Tower) and five daughters to marry off.

King Edward IV was, by all accounts, an intelligent, handsome man with great personal charm. But by 1470 his people were disillusioned with him. They had hoped for prosperity and peace – as the masses always do when a new prime minister or president is elected – and became frustrated when that didn't transpire. As the masses always do...

But the Yorkists became over confident – another theme we shall return to – and they released Henry VI from prison on the grounds of his good behaviour. Wacky, true, but good for him nonetheless.

And later that year, King Edward IV was forced to flee when his own nephew, John Neville, changed to the Lancastrian side and Henry VI was briefly restored to the throne of England.

How? Why?

They should never have allowed their enemy freedom. They lost control; they became complacent and thought he wouldn't fight back. But that's exactly what he did.

Henry VI had handled his adversity well. He'd behaved well, shown good leadership with his supporters and was able to take back the crown.

But the Yorkists triumphed in a surprise counter-attack less than a year later to regain power. Henry VI had only been back on the throne for six months.

Time for some serious foul play.

In April 1471 Edward entered the City of London in triumph. And within a month Henry VI mysteriously met his death in the Tower of London.

On his official death certificate the Yorkists declared he died of 'pure melancholy and displeasure'.

A world first.

At least the Yorkists had finished him off this time.

So what did happen to Henry VI in 1471? Well, eventually the skeleton was found to have been dismembered before being placed in a box – and not all the bones were present. Three much-worn teeth were found and the only piece of jaw present had lost its teeth before death. Most revealingly, his brown hair was found matted with blood on the skull, confirming that Henry VI had died as a result of a violent blow, possibly administered by Edward's younger brother, Richard.

Eighteen-year-old Richard is the only person named as being in the Tower on the night of May 21st 1471.

Bit of a giveaway.

So in 1471, Yorkist Edward IV was back on the throne. He was a popular murderer (it wasn't an oxymoron in those days) and had pretty much ordered the execution of every important Lancastrian but one – the teenager, Henry Tudor.

Henry's mother gave her son a bit of good advice – to leave the country for a short while, and leave he did.

For France.

For over a decade, licking his wounds and planning a Lancastrian come back. The young Henry was, of course, to make quite a comeback and father Henry VIII.

If you create enemies you create plots against you.

A lesson Anne Boleyn will ultimately learn.

King Edward IV was a notorious womaniser and his life of debauchery and self-indulgence ended in 1483. He died wealthy, respected and in his own bed after he'd caught a chill whilst out fishing.

Dying in your own bed was no mean feat for a 15th-century ruler. His son and heir, the 12-year-old Edward Junior, took over his father's role – minus the debauchery bit, obviously, and was proclaimed King Edward V. However, as is often the case with boy kings, his uncle Richard, Duke of Gloucester, had other ideas.

Cunningly, he proclaimed himself King Richard III.

His reign mirrored himself exactly.

Short, violent and extremely hairy.

But why did he feel the need to take the throne? Richard genuinely grieved for his brother, Edward, and he sent a nice copperplated handwritten letter of condolence to Queen Elizabeth, promising to do all that lay within his power to ensure the smooth succession of her son, Edward, now King Edward V.

But then he began thinking and pondered what the future held in store. He was 31 years of age with a distinguished career as a soldier already behind him. As the new king's uncle, he could expect to be prominent in the councils which governed the affairs of the land, and the future looked bright indeed.

Of course, he was immensely wealthy but he knew that at any moment his status could be taken away on the whim of his nephew. He could be brought low, his estates confiscated and then be forced into the ultimate sacrifice – made to marry a French girl still at junior school. Paranoia, avarice and fear of loss ensured he locked up the heir, the 12-year-old Edward Junior – and his brother Richard – in the Tower.

Richard III began to really believe he was omnipotent; more than just flesh and blood. He'd also created uncertainty with regard to the whereabouts of his nephews, disunity in the court and factions in the family.

In August 1485, the final battle of the Wars of the Roses took place in Market Bosworth between Richard III and Henry Tudor. Henry's mother was one of John of Gaunt's illegitimate children, Margaret Beaufort. Margaret was 12 years old when she married Henry's father, Edmund Tudor, and was pregnant by the time she was 13. They had been living together as man and wife – or boy and girl, strictly speaking – and when Edmund died in November 1456 she went to live with her brother-in-law, Henry VI, at Pembroke Castle. Before she'd hit 14 she had been married, widowed and given birth to a future king. Maybe that's what toughened her up for what was to come.

Time for a recap.

It's 1485. Six years before Henry VIII was to be born, his father, Lancastrian King Henry VII, a 28 year old who had been based in France for over a decade, decided to confront the Yorkists, based in London, by invading England via Milford Haven in South Wales. They then travelled up country to the fight venue somewhere in Shrewsbury.

To compound the problem, the 2,000 French mercenaries he brought with him spoke little English and were reluctant to ask for directions.

But Richard III was caught napping. He had men at Southampton to guard the south coast, some on the Essex coastline to defend the eastern border and some to hold the Tower in London.

Thinking he had all the bases covered, he relaxed and took himself off to Bosworth for a punch up with what he imagined would be a bedraggled assortment of a few dozen disenchanted Lancastrian supporters. So it came as a bit of a shock when he drew back his curtains on that fine summer's day to be confronted by Henry and 2,000 French lunatics.

Stunned by the news that they had arrived via Milford Haven and got straight through customs without a raised eyebrow, he barely had time to unleash his sword when he and his men were cut down in a flurry of mortal blows.

So, 108 years after the first minor quarrel, the man who was to be the father of Henry VIII was finally crowned Henry VII. Apart from the odd minor rebellion, the Wars of the Roses were all but over.

And the lesson to be learned from this final Battle of Bosworth?

Well, from a Lancastrian point of view, perseverance and a good plan are a powerful combination. But maybe get a SatNav next time. And the Yorkists should have never allowed themselves to become complacent. Plan for the unexpected and you won't be caught napping. It's a lesson we shall come back to again and again.

And again.

THE SECOND GOLDEN RULE:

BEWARE HUBRIS.

Hubris is a somewhat arrogant, extreme and foolish complacency. And the Yorkists showed exactly that in letting King Henry VI off the hook.

Winning competitors in the Ancient Greek Pythian Games in the 6th century BC – a forerunner of the Olympics – were given wreaths made of aromatic laurel leaves as a symbol of their triumph. And the expression 'Resting on your laurels' comes from that. Don't become complacent. And that was over 2,500 years ago

In this book we will continue to see many examples of hubris, from Henry VIII to Walter Raleigh to the head of security at Loch Leven where Mary, Queen of Scots was allowed to escape. One of the notable examples of hubris in British history was when a few hundred cavalrymen mounted a doomed charge against the Russian artillery; the aristocratic, self-centered competing generals, Lucan and Cardigan, appeared to have little concern for casualties but decided on the Charge of the Light Brigade in 1854.

Two hundred and forty-seven were left dead or wounded in the 'Valley of Death' at Balaclava whilst the two brother-in-laws, Lucan and Cardigan, watched on.

They survived.

Before *Titanic* set sail Captain E. J. Smith said: 'In all my experience, I have never been in any accident of any sort worth speaking about. I have seen but one vessel in distress in all my years at sea. I never saw a wreck and never have been wrecked nor was I ever in any predicament that threatened to end in disaster of any sort.'

He went down with the ship.

In the remarkable financial meltdown in the early part of this current century we saw how arrogant complacency meant thousands of ordinary people lost their investments and their livelihoods.

And hubris was at the root of collapse.

Back to the post-match analysis of Bosworth.

Following his victory Henry VII married Elizabeth, the daughter of his ex-enemy Edward IV. He did this partly to show there were no hard feelings and partly because she was tall, fair haired, and could speak perfect English, albeit with a Yorkshire accent. This act united the two houses that had been at war for many years, just as they had been united when the Yorkist King Edward IV married the Lancastrian Elizabeth Wydville. Keep your friends close and your enemies even closer.

To symbolise the union, Henry took as his emblem the Tudor Rose, which combined the white rose of York with a red rose of Lancashire. A nice conciliatory gesture.

Nine months after the marriage in 1486, the Queen had a son. They called him Arthur and the plan was he'd become king and we'll all live happily every after. But, as I'm sure you know, it didn't quite work out that way. The birth of Arthur was followed by a daughter, Margaret, destined to be queen of Scots.

And in 1491 – yes, we've got there – they had a second son and called him Henry.

Interestingly, the crown still owns land as a result of all the Wars of the Roses activity over 500 years ago. Our current Queen, as Duke of Lancaster, is a major Yorkshire landowner.

In over 30 years of the Wars of the Roses there were only 13 weeks of actual fighting, and more people died of plague than from battle wounds. But the memories of Towton have lived on.

There is something of a dearth of historical accounts of Henry VII's reign from 1485. It seems to fall between the two stools of being after the Wars of the Roses and the dramatic disappearance of the Princes in the Tower and before the main event of Henry VIII.

Even Shakespeare left him alone.

So before we look at Henry VIII's reign what can we learn from his father? As we've said, Henry VII was born in 1457 and the first 14 years of his life were spent in Wales.

He had been born after his father's death and his mother had remarried twice before he was 16. The next 14 years of his life were spent in France. Basically, when he came to the throne he'd spent very little time in England, knew hardly anyone in the country, had never managed anything, spoke French better than he did English and had no personal knowledge of government.

Fact is, he's the man who would decide that a young Spanish girl would marry his son and heir. And perhaps that's the biggest legacy he left.

But there is something else about Henry VII. William Wilberforce made a passing reference to him in his anti-slavery speech.

People look after themselves. Certainly Henry VII did.

And people look to have people around them who can also see the benefit – to themselves – in behaviour that should not be encouraged; behaviour that sometimes, on reflection, beggars belief.

History is full of powerful people who did some very bad things because no one was brave enough to stop them.

The next lesson comes directly from William Wilberforce's speech on the horrors of the slave trade in the House of Commons in 1789. He said, 'All that is necessary for the triumph of evil is that good men do nothing.' His view was that it was simply avarice that was the key motive for every monarch to go to war. If the king of Barbessin wanted brandy all he had to do was send his troops, in the night, to burn and desolate a village, with its captives then being used as commodities that could be bartered with British traders.

Whilst good men stood by.

Wilberforce said, 'What if I should be able to show this House that in a civilised part of Europe, in the time of our Henry VII, there were people who actually sold their own children? What if I should tell them that England itself was that country? What if I should point out to them that the very place where this inhumane traffic was carried out was the city of Bristol?'

In the reign of Henry VII, Ireland was used to drive a considerable trade in slaves with England. When a great plague infested the Irish they believed the plague was a punishment sent from heaven for the sin of the slave trade, and therefore abolished it. They only stopped it when they truly believed there was a message from on high.

Wilberforce asked if any man could contradict 'the dictates of his conscience, the principles of justice, the laws of religion, and of God'. Even when they could no longer plead ignorance bad men would continue to feather their nest until 'a few good men' became a cabal and grew.

And the abolition of slavery began with a few good men with a conscience believing that a wrong could – and should – be put right.

And the lesson we can learn is clear:

All it needs for evil to triumph is that a few good people do nothing.

The rest of Henry VII's reign was fairly uneventful. Needless to say he had gone down the rather traditional and well-worn route of declaring war on France but even that ended in a damp squib and he eventually agreed to withdraw for a cheap bribe.

But it's he who decided who Henry VIII should marry.

CHAPTER 3

'Yikes, it's Katie', Pavlov's Dogs and the Third Golden Rule

Marrying young French girls was considered rather passé in the early part of the 16th century so Henry VII decided that his eldest son, the future King Arthur should marry a Spanish princess. This considerably narrowed his selection but finally he chose the king of Spain's daughter, Katherine of Aragon.

Pacing nervously up and down the quayside at Portsmouth awaiting his new bride's arrival, the first-born son of Henry VII, young Arthur, looked forward to Katherine of Aragon's lithe, olive-skinned body and typically Spanish long, dark locks.

So, as you might imagine, there was a good deal of cursing and looking to the Heavens in disbelief – as the pale-skinned, grey-eyed, strawberry blonde Katie cleared immigration and stepped out into the English sunlight for the very first time. 'Yikes!' was the first word she heard from Arthur, yet to his credit, he never explained this term to her. Unfortunately, this meant she spent the rest of her life greeting everyone she met by taking a sharp step backwards and exclaiming, 'Yikes!'

They were married ten days later on November 14th 1501 at St Paul's Cathedral. He was 15 and she was 16. Only 16. But he loved her so. She was too young to fall in love and I can't quite remember the rest of the lyric.

There are no guarantees in life. And in particular, when it comes to mail-order brides, you pays yer money, you takes yer choice, and there are seldom any refunds.

Due to the inclement December weather and the general mayhem surrounding the Christmas shopping period, Katie and Art – as the tabloids would no doubt these days dub them – postponed their honeymoon until they were old enough to have sex the following spring. They chose Ludlow Castle in Wales and booked in for a long weekend.

Now we've all experienced wet weekends in Wales, but the nightmare for our young lovers proved far worse. Day one, he sneezed, day two, she sneezed. Day three, he wheezed and coughed, day four, she wheezed and coughed. Day five, they couldn't go home because they were both too ill.

And it's worth asking a question right now that becomes absolutely critical many years later. Sir Antony Willoughby – a body servant of Arthur's – was subsequently asked to tell what the teenage Arthur had said to him whilst sneezing and coughing on the morning after the night before at Ludlow Castle. He apparently bragged to Sir

Anthony, 'Last night I was in Spain!' Was this just teenage bravado or a true statement of accomplishment?

And did anybody remember this properly anyway?

Our recollection of events is more fallible than we realise. The idea that we remember where we were when we heard of a huge news 'event', for example, is a common one. The top three for many being the death of the Princess of Wales, 9/11 and the assassination of John F. Kennedy. But this idea that we have a 'flashbulb memory' is just plain wrong. People can't remember accurately what they were doing when they heard about the Berlin wall coming down or when man landed on the moon.

They just *think* they can.

There was a study conducted in America on the day after 9/11 whereby people were asked what they were doing when they first heard about the Twin Towers. And then, one, six or 32 weeks later the same subjects were asked to recall the event again.

And the longer the gap before they were asked again, the less consistent their memory and the more false details – vivid but wrong – were added. They were totally confident that their memory of 9/11 was right. But they weren't recalling 9/11 more accurately, they were just more confident about their inaccurate memory.

President George W. Bush was reading to school children when he was informed that a second plane had hit the

Twin Towers and that America was under attack. Yet he has twice publicly recalled that before entering the classroom he had watched on television as the first plane hit the tower. And although that's not possible it's led to conspiracy theories. Fact is, he can no longer remember where he was. He just thinks he can. We all do it.

The next lesson for us all is clear – your memory is reliably unreliable. That's why you shouldn't always believe what people tell you.

But back in 1971 I *was* outside the main hall at Ashton Grammar School waiting for the Physics exam...

Anyway, Katherine and Arthur were married for a good few months. Two horny teenagers in a damp and cold castle; was the marriage not consummated or was it under the covers and whoopsy daisy?

Either way, day six, he sneezed again. Day seven, he wheezed and coughed again. You get the idea.

Day 107, he croaked. I don't know about you, but I'd want my money back.

And that's how Henry VIII (born on June 28th 1491) became first in line to the throne.

Let's summarise Spanish Katie's position at this point. She's 16 years old and has been living in a foreign land for less than a year. She's met a 15-year-old prince and married him within a fortnight. From day one, she believes

Yikes is the customary greeting in England. And when she finally gets to grips with the cold weather, the language and the greasy breakfasts, she finds herself widowed. How could things possibly get worse? Well, how about if your father-in-law decides that you should now marry your dead husband's 11-year-old brother? That's got to come pretty high up.

Eleven!

I am not making this up.

This required the Pope (Julius II if you are interested; that becomes important later on too) to grant a dispensation based on the fact that her marriage to Arthur was never actually consummated due to his obsession with fly fishing and what with all the brass monkey weather in Wales and all. Suppressing a wry smile which some even described as a snigger, the Pope duly obliged, wishing her better luck next time and encouraging her to hide her new husband's rods.

Sensibly, the hapless couple – sorry, the happy couple – waited a while before tying the knot. They wanted to make sure that the ceremony was a really joyful occasion and so they naturally waited until Henry VII died. And it gave Henry VIII a chance to grow up a bit too.

But there was another reason they waited for Henry VII's death. Also included in the papal dispensation for his younger son to marry his brother's widow was a proviso that allowed Henry VII himself to marry his widowed daughter-in-law.

If he wanted to.

Cheeky bugger.

Henry VII is about to draw his last breath.

Time for the third Golden Rule.

It's natural. It's in the Bible (Galatians 6:7–10) and is the immutable law of karma. Indeed, it's at the very heart of most ancient religions and faiths such as Hinduism, Buddhism, Shintoism and Confucianism. And it's as relevant now as it's ever been.

THE THIRD GOLDEN RULE:

YOU REAP WHAT YOU SOW.

Throughout the Wars of the Roses we saw time and time again how the behaviour of each king and so many of his cohorts came back to bite them.

They kept losing but also lost the lessons they could and should have learned. So much unnecessary bloodshed. So little consideration for others.

If you plant corn, you don't get potatoes.

If you do, take it up with whoever supplied the seeds.

For every action there is a reaction; a result. If you gossip, you're likely to lose friends. If you lie, you'll become known as untrustworthy and lacking integrity. If you make others happy through service, charity and kind acts, you sow happiness like a seed, and it will give you the fruit of happiness. If you make others unhappy through harsh words, insult, ill-treatment or cruelty, you sow unhappiness like a seed, and you too will eventually suffer misery and unhappiness. That's why the purpose of life is to develop loving relationships and make a meaningful, positive contribution.

The expression 'Treat others as you would like them to treat you' is often at the heart of the world's greatest religions and philosophies. It's seen as the foundation upon which decency and morality are based.

But it has a flaw.

Sometimes people treat you in a way which is acceptable to them but *you* have higher expectations.

It's why we need to ask people what is important to them, to ask what their expectations are and to ask what we can improve on in all our relationships.

But we can't always treat people how *they* want to be treated – exemplified by a relationship we will study towards the end of the book. If Elizabeth I had treated Mary, Queen of Scots as *she* would have wanted to be treated, Mary would have had freedom and the crown. If we treated all the bad guys like they would want to be treated, there'd be anarchy. In rivalries it's often judicious to treat people how you think they should be treated in your best interests. I'm always flabbergasted when I go on tours around sports stadiums to find the away dressing rooms are not well decorated and furnished. No hooks to hang clothes, cramped conditions and small showers and so on – all to make the opposition angry. For me that's the opposite psychology I'd recommend. In my away dressing rooms there'd be soothing music, relaxing areas and first-class comfort. I'd want my sporting rivals to come out on to the field serene, laid-back and nonchalant...

But, as we will discover later in this chapter, those who follow 'Treat others as you would like them to treat you' will tend to be happier, wealthier, have better relation-ships, achieve more in their careers and lead more reward-ing lives than those who don't.

Because you reap what you sow.

Most parents are aware that a teacher's expectations of a child become self-fulfilling prophecies. If a teacher believes them to be slow, the child will believe that too and indeed learn slowly. The lucky child who strikes a teacher as bright will pick up on their expectation and rise to fulfil it. This finding has been confirmed so many times, and in such varied settings, that it's no longer even debated.

It turns out that self-fulfilling prophecies are just as preva-lent in offices as they are in elementary school classrooms.

If a manager is convinced that the people in their charge are first-rate, they'll reliably outperform a group whose manager believes the opposite – even if the innate talent of the two groups is similar.

Focus special attention on an employee's first year – because that's when expectations are set. Make sure new employees get matched with outstanding supervisors and are 'buddied' with excellent people. And don't forget to set high expectations for yourself.

In George Bernard Shaw's – *Pygmalion* – Eliza Doolittle explains. 'You see, really and truly, apart from the things anyone can pick up – the dressing and the proper way of speaking, and so on – the difference between a lady and a flower girl is not how she behaves but how she's treated. I shall always be a flower girl to Professor Higgins because he always treats me as a flower girl and always will. But I know I can be a lady to you because you always treat me as a lady and always will.'

Some managers naturally treat their subordinates in a way that leads to superior performance. Encouraging and cajoling, praising where praise is due and setting them tasks that help them to develop their skills and talent. But most managers are like Professor Higgins. It may be unintentional, but often they treat subordinates as substandard, setting them lower targets than they are capable of achieving which leads naturally to lower performance.

In short, what a manager expects of an employee, and the way they treat them, largely determines the employee's performance and career progress. Expect great things and you're much more likely to get great things. Expect very little and you'll get just that.

You reap what you sow.

Of course, that doesn't explain all the successful people whose school report said they would never amount to much. They are the exceptions to the rule and usually turn out to be exceptionally talented in ways not possible to detect in their youth.

The idea that we can become conditioned to react in a certain way isn't a new one. Over a hundred years ago Russian psychologist Ivan Pavlov demonstrated this with his famous experiment that he called 'The Ivan Pavlov Canine Conditioning Experiment'. Unfortunately, the publisher of his paper thought this a little too long and cumbersome and persuaded him to change the title to the much shorter and catchier 'Pavlov's Dogs' adding to a slightly put out Pavlov, 'You'll thank me for it in the long run.'

In his experiment, Pavlov placed food on one side of a room and some hungry dogs on the other. When the dogs got a whiff of the food, they began to salivate and Pavlov rang a bell. He repeated this enough times to create an anchor between the bell ringing and the dogs salivating. Finally, he placed no food in the room and just rang the bell. And despite not a crumb of food being present, the dogs would salivate. He'd successfully conditioned them into behaving a certain way. Then they attacked him.

Only kidding.

It is the same with humans. A touch, a tone of voice or even a look can induce a certain state in us. The sound of a firework can bring back terrifying memories for war veterans. An incident in a swimming pool can make some people afraid of water for life.

So can you use this information to your advantage in business? Well, if you bring to mind a time when you achieved an exceptional performance, you can use it as an anchor to create another exceptional performance. Here's the proof of the Pavlova. I mean, pudding.

Back in the early 60s, when we in Britain were learning to swing, driving Minis around town, and dabbling in hallucinogenics, the Russians were doing experiments on their top athletes with a view to world domination. As far as running, jumping and throwing went, at least.

To prove that simply *visualising* a great performance could lead to one, they divided their athletes into two groups. One was sent off to a special camp where they trained exceptionally hard for a month. Let's call them the short straw athletes. I say that because the other group were ordered not to train at all. Instead, all they had to do was sit at home and 'visualise' a great performance. A month later, the two groups went head to head in competition and the athletes who had done nothing more than visualise a great performance won hands down. Russia's domination of track and field in the 60s and 70s was thought to be partly the result of using this technique.

Not to be outdone, the Americans decided to test this theory for themselves. Dr Blaslotto at the University of Chicago set up an experiment with basketball players. He divided them into three groups and recorded their success at shooting baskets when given a number of free shots. Each group were then given different instructions and told to come back in 30 days' time. One group was told not to practise free shots at all; one group was told to practise free shots every day; and the third group was told to practise free shots only in their mind by *visualising* a successful shot.

A month later the groups were tested again and the results compared to their initial performance. Perhaps not surprisingly, the first group who had not practised at all showed no improvement whatsoever. However, the second group, who had been asked to practise, showed an improvement of over 20% in their successful shots. Again, not surprising since practice makes perfect, right? So what about the third group who had just been sitting at home, eating pretzels, drinking cola and watching daytime television? Well, remarkably, they too recorded an improved performance level of over 20%. I know what you're thinking; that sounds like my kind of training regime too.

The ability to do great things, to literally change the world, always comes from within. The essential element is invisible to the eye. So it's not enough to just treat others as you wish to be treated or behave as you wish others to behave towards you. You have to behave as you wish to be *perceived*.

The best way to predict the future is to invent it yourself. Don't just wait to see what turns up; decide what you want and then make it happen if you want to be truly happy.

Try this exercise. Write down where you think you will be ten years from now. Detail things like where you will live, the kind of house you will live in, the kind of car you will drive, how your family has developed, how much money you will have and, most importantly, how and why you are satisfied doing what you have decided to do. There's a good chance that you will come very close to achieving what you write down. Because the best way to predict the future is to invent it.

According to a 2007 survey by the University of Chicago amongst workers in America, the clergy are the happiest and most satisfied in their jobs. A whopping 87% reported being 'very satisfied'. And they wouldn't lie. Firefighters came second with an 80% satisfaction rate. In fact, all of the top ten most satisfying jobs were professions that involved caring for, teaching or protecting others. Jobs that polled satisfaction rates of 60% or more included education administrators, painters and sculptors, teachers, authors, psychologists, special education teachers, and operating engineers.

Another study released by the Institute for Research on Unlimited Love and conducted by such top universities as Harvard and Chicago, has also found that the happiest people are those who either give to or help others on a regular basis. They all treat others as they would like to be treated themselves and they reap what they sow.

Least happy in the survey were petrol pump attendants. And not just because they're forever out on the forecourts changing the prices. People don't treat them well. They don't feel important. They don't feel what they are doing is especially worthwhile. And their two basic psychological needs are left unfulfilled.

Even though we may spend a lot of time looking up to them, roofers didn't fair too well either. Having a roof fixed can be an expensive business but it's not something that is admired when it's finished. We have a basic psychological need to be loved and a basic psychological need to be important; to feel that what we are doing is worthwhile. If you want to get the best out of someone you need to let them know you truly care about them and appreciate the efforts they go to.

Particularly your children.

Treat others as you wish to be treated and you will be happier and more successful.

Do something kind or good without expecting anything in return.

Or, to quote from the Bible again, 'Cast your bread upon the waters.'

Robert Emmons from the University of California and Michael McCullough from the University of Miami have done a number of studies on gratitude. They regard it as the 'forgotten factor' in happiness research. Psychologists and scientists are latecomers to the concept of gratitude; religions and philosophers have pretty much always embraced gratitude as an integral component of health and general well-being. Being told what you are good at and being grateful actually affects your health and general well-being. Grateful individuals place less importance on material goods and are less envious of other people. So tell people what you think they're really good at. Be sincere, honest and genuine. And better still, tell them when there are other people around. Cast your bread upon the waters – you will reap what you sow.

Treat others as you wish to be treated is a lesson the kings of England could and should have learned.

A lesson J. Bruce Ismay should have learned too. In the event, he made it off *Titanic* whilst so many perished. He said afterwards, 'I just kind of fell into the lifeboat.' If he had treated others as he wished to be treated himself he wouldn't have changed the design of the ship and reduced the number of lifeboats to a pitiful number. He wouldn't have put Chief Officer, William Murdoch, through the embarrassment of being demoted to First Officer; of Charles Lightoller, the First Officer being demoted to Second Officer; and Second Officer David Blair having to leave the ship.

With the key to the locker in the crow's nest tucked in his pocket.

Which meant that on the night of April 14th – 1912 the lookout on the crow's nest on *Titanic*, Fred Fleet, did not have binoculars to help him see icebergs.

You reap what you sow.

Henry VII presumably had had second thoughts during the seven years from Arthur's death to his own demise about marrying his son's young widow and never did remarry.

Henry VIII became king on the death of his father Henry VII in 1509.

It's Henry VIII's show now.

CHAPTER 4

Henry's 'Great Matter', Misplaced Expectations and the Four-Minute mile

When Henry VIII was crowned king, Thomas More wrote in a poem that was presented to Henry at his coronation: 'This day is the end of our slavery, the fount of our liberty; the end of sadness and the beginning of joy.'

Sounds like Margaret Thatcher in May 1979. Strictly speaking she paraphrased St. Francis of Assisi, 'Where there is discord, may we bring harmony', etc., but the misplaced expectation is all there. And again like the sort of thing Tony Blair said in May 1997. In May 2010 Cameron said, 'I want to try and build a more responsible society. Those who can should and those who can't we will always help'. Theresa May in 2016 said, 'We need a government that will deliver serious social reform and make ours a country that truly works for everyone.' Boris said, 'The time has come to act, to take decisions, to give strong leadership and to change this country for the better' when on the steps of 10 Downing Street in July 2019.

Misplaced expectation.

And who held the important title of 'Squire of the Body' and walked along in the king's funeral procession, clad in his newly issued black livery?

None other than Thomas Boleyn. Already scheming to achieve higher status through his own political efforts or by using his children. His youngest daughter, Anne, was eight at the time.

When she was 12 years old in 1513, Anne Boleyn left England to be a maid of honour in Brussels. Not quite France but near enough. And the purpose of her leaving these shores was to be 'finished'.

It's called a gap year now.

She was to live abroad for nine years. Quite a bit of finishing needed obviously. Thomas Boleyn's decision to send his daughter to Belgium and work for Margaret of Austria was presumably prompted by the opportunities created by working abroad; learning a language or two and a bit of music and dance. It would do wonders for her prospects on her return.

It is easy to underestimate the importance of entertainment in those days. The work ethic is all well and good but once leisure is plentiful, managing it becomes a serious business. Ask anyone who's a member of a golf club that is owned by the members. Or on the committee of the local working men's club. We all have a need to be important and if we don't get that through work we turn our attention to seeking a position in a voluntary capacity. Beware the motives of people who do.

Everyone has a need to be important; to feel that what they are doing is worthwhile. If you employ people, treat everyone you employ as a volunteer. It's a lesson we should all learn.

We will obviously hear more of the Boleyns later in the book.

Back to 1509 and Henry VIII's coronation.

With the Wars of the Roses a distant memory and Katherine now used to English breakfasts, the 18-year-old Henry VIII became king in the spring of 1509. And, with his father having not taken up his 'option' he is able to marry the 23-year-old Spanish girl in June 1509 – known to her ladies-in-waiting as 'Katherine of Arrogant'.

Yikes.

Surprisingly, the marriage between Henry VIII and Katherine seems to have started as a happy one. In the first few years of marriage he commissioned the – *Mary Rose* – the flagship of the Navy – and focused on warring with France. By now that's a basic expectation for a king of England he's learned from his forefathers.

He busied himself being king, and being busy means you spend less time doing things that don't need doing. When we come to the fifth Golden Rule we will look at the downside of doing things that are neither important nor urgent. It's widely thought that it was Chaucer in the 12th century who called idle hands the Devil's tools, and maybe that's a lesson that Henry should have learned. As any good parent knows, if you keep your kids busy doing worthwhile things they don't have time to get up to mischief.

In September 2008, 25 people were killed when a Metrolink commuter train crashed head-on into a Union Pacific freight train in Los Angeles, California. It is thought that the Metrolink train ran through a red signal while the conductor was busy text messaging.

He was texting for goodness' sake.

Wrongful death lawsuits caused $500 million in losses for Metrolink.

In the UK over 1,000 people are killed as a result of car accidents each year and one out of every four is caused by 'distractions'. Texting while driving is six times more likely to cause an accident than driving drunk. Answering a text takes away your attention for about five seconds. Travelling at 55 mph, that's enough time to travel the length of a football field.

It's called work for a reason. Whatever you are doing you should do your absolute best.

You should concentrate.

Particularly if people's lives are on the line.

– Portmanteau – words have already been coined for people not even focused on walking around. The 'phubber' snubs physical contact in favour of his or her phone. And there's the 'smombie', the smartphone zombie so fascinated by their device that they are oblivious to the world around them.

The smombie has become one of the principal obstacles to normal passage around a modern city. So much so that in both China and Hawaii there are laws that mean using a smartphone or tablet while crossing the street can land you with a fine.

We shouldn't need a law for common sense but maybe it's coming...

Anyway, Henry and Katherine had their ups and downs like all couples do, but generally things went pretty much according to plan for the first ten years or so. Until, that was, Henry had his mid-life crisis which in those days kicked in before you got to your thirties. The rejection of Katherine appears to have begun shortly after the seven year itch, a movie made famous over 400 years later by Marilyn Monroe standing over a grid with a white dress on. They had had a son, born on New Year's Day 1511 and named Henry, but he died at less than eight weeks old. It was to prove to be a turning point in British history. Of course, they did have a daughter, Mary, in 1516. But male ego gets in the way and he wants a son.

Three years after Mary was born, Henry VIII's affair with his teenage mistress, Elizabeth Blount, had led to the birth of his illegitimate son, Henry Fitzroy. Young Henry was born at the Priory of St Lawrence at Blackmore, Essex, in June 1519. And Henry was ecstatic. He was not only full of paternal pride as Henry Fitzroy had more than a passing resemblance to himself; he was also looking at evidence that not only was he capable of producing a fine, healthy heir, but that his Spanish Queen could not.

Basically it wasn't his fault. There was something wrong with her or the marriage.

And perhaps this was the real turning point. The point at which Henry VIII believed he could father a healthy boy but not by Katherine.

And once he believed that he looked for evidence to support his belief.

A lesson that a certain sub-four-minute miler could and should have learned back in 1954.

When you ask people to name the first man to run a mile in less than four minutes even people born well after 1954 can tell you it was Roger Bannister. On May 6th 1954 at the Iffley Road track in Oxford the 25-year-old British medical student became the first man to run a mile in less than four minutes. In 3 minutes 59.4 seconds to be precise. And, of course, to beat someone else's world record.

But ask people to name the man who was the world record holder up to that point or, indeed, to name the next man to run the mile in under four minutes – and beat Bannister's time – most people struggle.

In December 1953, in Melbourne, Australian John Landy had set a new Australian Mile Record of four minutes 2 seconds, equalling Roger Bannister's Empire Record, set earlier in the year. After the race, he predicted he would never run a four-minute mile. 'If I do so before I retire from serious competition, it will be only luck,' said Landy. Since July 1945 the world record for the mile had been held by Sweden's Gunder Hagg, who was affectionately known as 'Gunder the Wonder'. He had set the new world mile mark of four 4 minutes 1.4 seconds.

Gunder's record had stood for a full nine years and yet just 46 days after Bannister achieved the feat, Landy achieved a time of 3 minutes 58 seconds – on June 21st 1954 in Turku, Finland. Landy had improved by more than three seconds in one race and taken the world record off Bannister. The second man to do so.

Landy held the world record for over three years until, on July 19th 1957, Yorkshireman Derek Ibbotson posted a time of 3 minutes 57.2 seconds.

Landy had not believed it was possible. It was only when desire and real belief came together that there was then a conviction.

Bannister simply believed he could do it and put a comprehensive plan together to achieve it. The previous world record holder had held the record for nine years; the holder *after* Bannister held the record for three years. Bannister was world record holder for less than two months.

But he's the one who got knighted. He's the one we remember.

The lesson that John Landy should have learned from Henry VIII is that you don't always need hard evidence that something can be done before you plan to do it. It just seems that way.

Don't just set your goals when you have 'know-how' – sometimes set them with no 'how?'

Henry VIII had been unhappy with Katherine – his bride of some ten years – and needless to say she's unhappy with him as Henry made his illegitimate son Earl of Nottingham *and* Duke of Richmond and Somerset. He went on to also give his son several other important posts including Lord High Admiral of England when he was only six years old. He later became a Knight of the Garter.

The queen firmly put her foot down when Henry wanted to appoint his son king of Ireland. Henry admitted defeat on that one but still made the boy Lord Lieutenant of Ireland.

After the birth of his son, Henry had a number of affairs whilst his marriage was on a one way ticket to nowhere. And he turned his attention to Anne Boleyn after discarding her sister, Mary Carey, having previously added the girls' mother to his list of sexual conquests.

What was Mary Boleyn thinking when she got married to Bill Carey in 1520? Mary Carey. It's a bit like Oprah Winfrey marring Deepak Chopra and becoming Oprah Chopra.

Memorable though.

The chronology and pattern of royal grants to William and Mary Carey suggest that Mary's affair with the king started shortly after she married. And there were very significant grants to William Carey in 1524 and 1526 when Mary had children. He seems to have been rewarded particularly well for his compliant role as nominal father to the king's bastards. By all accounts Henry VIII would not have countenanced sharing the sexual favours of any of his mistresses, even if they did have a husband; he required chastity from his sexual partners.

But she had served a purpose and her younger sister Anne was the next young woman now in focus.

Henry VIII had fallen well and truly in love.

Among the impressive pieces of evidence we have about how Henry VIII felt about Anne are the 17 letters he wrote around 1528. Ten of them in French and seven in English, which is impressive in itself.

And we repeat a lesson from when Henry IV put it in writing that he was going to have Richard II bumped off.

Never write down the words 'I love you'. You can always deny you said it. You cannot retract what you write.

Henry's conviction that he could have a divorce from Katherine in order to marry Anne Boleyn comes from his view that in the Bible (Leviticus 20:21) it clearly states, 'If a man shall take his brother's wife, it is an unclean thing...he shall be without children.' Much is made of this but the piece was obviously in the Bible when he married Katherine all those years ago, and they got a dispensation from the Pope as they argued her marriage to Henry's brother wasn't consummated.

As my mother used to say, 'You can't have your cake and eat it too.'

Lesson? If the lawyers get involved, check the small print. If Henry's right then Pope Clement VII has to accept there has been a papal mistake, they've exceeded their own powers and he'll have to eat his words. And people don't like doing that.

The key thing here is that Henry really and truly believed in his side and the Pope thinks like my mum; you can't have your cake and eat it. Once that happens there are going to be tears.

As in businesses, factions are part of the scenery. It is easy to dismiss factions as backbiting, bitching and seeking self-advantage but it is to miss the point. And often, the prize. Factions are the form politics and businesses take when their focus is the will of one man. In this case, Henry.

Look at the stories of Hitler, the Byzantium, Roman and British empires and Stalinist Moscow. More latterly Idi Amin, Saddam Hussain and Robert Mugabe. I could go on. If direct opposition to the omnipotent one is impossible, rebels become conspirators.

Anne Boleyn had gone the direct route and gained the king's favour. And that means losers and that, in turn, means conspirators. And if there are factions, people are not focused on the common goal.

So here's the next lesson.

If you run a business or manage a team, keep people focused on the common goal and don't allow them to get distracted.

Companies are at their most successful when people are focused on the common goal. Factions make people face inwards and eventually everyone can lose. The expression 'Live by the sword, die by the sword' should in Anne's case be reworded 'Gain power by seeking favour with one man and beware the ramifications when you fall out of favour.' Anne Boleyn's subsequent fall was a consequence of her allies eventually recalculating in the most calculating way when she produced no son and Henry's head was turned by Jane Seymour.

For now though, in 1525, there's a battle royal developing between Anne Boleyn, her naturally conspiratorial father and the king's loyal servant and confidant for many years, Cardinal Wolsey. Meanwhile the Spanish king, Charles I, is winning a war with Francis I of France.

Cardinal Wolsey, in turn, is entering a battle between himself and the Pope as he has been charged by Henry with the responsibility of getting the king a divorce from Katherine. Or at least an annulment. The papacy was a job that Wolsey had coveted for years. And Katherine is unhappy that Wolsey is constantly between her and her husband. Frankly, she's hopping mad and infuriated with the cardinal.

And Anne's unhappy with the cardinal too. And Anne's dad. And the Pope. And, pretty soon, Henry himself. You couldn't make this up, could you? The cardinal is between a rock and a number of hard places. For once his reach seems to have exceeded his grasp.

To complicate things further, Henry VIII has two sisters who are not raving fans of Wolsey either.

Henry's sister, Margaret Tudor, was two years older than the king and had married King James IV of Scotland 20 years before. But James had died in a battle against the English ten years into their marriage (Margaret will eventually become grandmother of Mary, Queen of Scots, which becomes relevant later in the book if you're still with me). Less than a year after her husband died, in 1514, Margaret married Archibald Douglas. Despite being Earl of Angus, he was an England supporter so she was removed from the regency and exiled to England. But, as is often the case when people see greener grass on the other side of the fence, Margaret rather quickly changed allegiances and supported the pro-French regent, John Stewart, the Duke of Albany. She won an annulment from Douglas, and then married Henry Stewart.

Basically she's got an agenda for her son, James.

Henry's other sister, Mary Tudor, had been born some five years after Henry. She had been betrothed to Katherine of Aragon's nephew, Charles (by now the Holy Roman Emperor) but, surprise, surprise, there'd been a fallout and some misunderstandings between Spain, the Holy Roman Empire and France, and so Henry cancelled the betrothal.

Mary probably had no desire to marry a French boy four years younger than herself, but it got worse in that Henry's choice for a replacement was 34 years older – King Louis XII of France, described as 'feeble and pocky'.

By all accounts Mary was an attractive woman and in love with Henry's friend, Charles Brandon, the Duke of Suffolk. So, weeping, sulking and with a long face, the 18 year old went off to France in 1514 and married the 52-year-old king of France, with the Boleyn sisters, Anne and Mary, wiping her tears for her. Whatever Mary did with him and for him, she did a grand job and Louis XII died on New Year's Day 1515, after just three months of marriage.

Good news or bad news? Well, she's lost the husband she didn't want to marry but her future is now uncertain.

Everybody gets bad news and it makes us all feel sad and depressed. But then, after a while, a funny thing happens. We don't feel quite so bad. Did you read about the guy who mistakenly threw away a £100,000 winning scratch card? Naturally, he was gutted at the time. But now he's probably having a good laugh about it.

Or maybe not.

However, for most of us – and certainly for Mary – bad news often turns out to be nothing like as devastating as we first feared. Why is that? Well, a study by Daniel Gilbert at Harvard University has come up with a theory. To test it, he set up a series of classic social psychology studies that most people would be familiar with: going for a job interview and getting rejected. Of course, as with all these experiments, things weren't quite what they seemed. Firstly, all the interviewees were led to believe there was an actual job on offer. Then they were asked to complete a questionnaire which included a section about how they would feel if they didn't get it. To quantify their disappointment, they were asked to predict the change in their mood on a scale of 1 to 10, where 10 was happy at getting the job. All agreed that their mood would worsen by two points to 8 if they were rejected. One woman, who'd arrived in a bit of a mood anyway, said it could drop to 4, rise to 8, drop to 4 again, and then she'd probably thump someone.

Naturally, nobody was offered the job. What Gilbert was interested in was their reaction to the bad news and, in particular, how this differed from their prediction. But there was another little twist in the tail. Half the group was interviewed by just one person, and half by a panel of three. This made it easier for those rejected by one person to rationalise the decision as just one person's preference.

But for those who were rejected by three people it was naturally more difficult to dismiss, since this was seemingly a considered judgement by a panel.

The results showed that, immediately after the rejection, those interviewed by just one person could rationalise the decision and their good mood only fell by 0.4 of a point, whereas the ones rejected by the panel of three saw their mood drop further, to 1.25, but still not as low as they had predicted. On being told that it was all an experiment and there was never any job on offer, the woman who'd threatened to thump someone overturned the desk, set fire to the curtains and stormed out.

So why is it that we don't feel quite so bad as we thought we would? Well, we all have an in-built psychological immune system that recalibrates our perception of the world and our feelings. So whenever life kicks us in the unmentionables, the psychological immune system gets to work rationalising what's happened and, over time, stopping it hurting as much as we feared. Of course, that's still no excuse to start a conga at your granny's funeral, but at least now you know why it wasn't so bad after all.

Not only did Mary soon get over the bad news of losing her husband, she married Charles Brandon before her brother could marry her off to a Spanish prince. Henry was not best pleased but Mary and Charles named their first child, born in 1515, Henry.

Astute move, Charlie.

Mary was a good friend of her sister-in-law Katherine of Aragon, and was a supporter of hers in the 'Great Matter' of the divorce, and she rejected Anne Boleyn. So Wolsey had Charles and Mary to contend with too.

It's like working for a family business but not being part of the family as far as Wolsey's concerned.

At least Cardinal Wolsey's made himself rich, famous and important whilst he's been doing the king's bidding. Rumour is he's been embezzling and funding his colleges at Oxford University where he took his degree at the age of 15. He probably has as many illegitimate children as Henry VIII himself. He's got himself the positions of Archbishop and Lord Chancellor and has his own abbey in St Albans.

However, to make things more complicated for Wolsey, in May 1527, the Hapsburg troops have ransacked Rome and imprisoned Pope Clement VII. He'd chosen the wrong horse to back and sided with France in the League of Cognac.

This is not, as you might suspect, a competition involving brandy drinking.

It's time to recap who's who and what's what in the summer of 1527.

The king of Spain is Charles I. He is also Holy Roman Emperor, Charles V. He is Belgian-born but of Spanish descent. His maternal grandparents are the parents of Katherine of Aragon who, in 1527, is still Henry VIII's wife.

The king of England is Henry VIII. He has shifted his support from Spain to France yet wants to divorce his Spanish, Catholic wife of 18 years in order to marry Anne Boleyn.

Cardinal Wolsey – the king of England's loyal number two – is trying to restore peace in Europe and also endeavouring to get Pope Clement VII to agree to Henry divorcing Katherine of Aragon whilst he (the Pope) is entirely under the thumb of his captor, Charles V, who is Katherine's nephew.

In the three-year period from 1527 to Wolsey's eventual demise in 1530 the political shenanigans puts what happens in most companies in the present day well in the shade.

The French have a lovely expression: *Plus ça change, plus c'est la même chose*, which loosely translates as 'The more things change, the more they remain the same'. Of course, they have ones even lovelier than that but just not as appropriate to this part of the book. But all things do change.

All things pass.

And that's a useful lesson for us.

One thousand years before this the Greek philosopher Heraclitus of Ephesus was the one saying that 'you cannot bath twice in the same river' because the river always runs and changes. So it is for everything else. All things change and in the end pass away. It's the reason we shouldn't worry about things as much as we all do.

However good or bad a situation is, it will change. And so will our perception of it.

Wolsey had been all powerful during the early part of Henry's reign. He had been his right-hand man and facilitator; his political manoeuvres were legendary. He had seen mistresses come and go. Indeed, he had fixed for many attractive young women to be brought to the king's bed chambers and organised for the various illegitimate offspring of Henry to be born quietly and their mothers cared for.

But he's made enemies as he plotted and schemed to his own advantage.

Wolsey had assumed that Anne would become nothing more than the king's mistress and that if the king were to marry again it would be to a French queen.

Wolsey hasn't treated Anne as he would wish to be treated himself – and he's about to pay the price.

CHAPTER 5

The Pot Bull, Aunty Dot and Lady Wallop

So why did the Pope refuse to give Henry his divorce? Why was Wolsey unsuccessful?

Well, it's not just that the Pope's in the pocket of Henry's wife's nephew. The two sides have reached a stand-off. Edward Fox, Doctor of Divinity, and Stephen Gardiner, Doctor of both civil and canon law, had unsuccessfully gone to Rome on the instructions of both Henry and Wolsey to convince the Pope to grant Cardinal Wolsey the power to rule on the king's case. And the Pope knew what that ruling would be.

In April 1528, Pope Clement agreed to send the Italian Cardinal Lorenzo Campeggio to England to 'try' the case with Cardinal Wolsey, but did not agree to give either cardinal the power to pronounce sentence. Cardinal Campeggio arrived in England at the end of September in the same year and the 'proceedings', such as they were, began the following month. Cardinal Campeggio had come with the rather unhelpful suggestion that Henry reconcile with the queen – which went down like the proverbial lead balloon.

Complicating the situation somewhat, Anne Boleyn and her ever-helpful father suggested to King Henry that Cardinal Wolsey was not really doing his absolute best to obtain the annulment. And there's a pot bull involved too.

The Italian cardinal had brought with him the ornamental bull that authorised him to adjudicate on the case. So the king kept nagging Cardinal Wolsey to get the bull from Cardinal Campeggio, without success.

Early the following year the Pope became conveniently ill, so the court didn't convene until May. During the interval, Cardinal Wolsey had been doing what he could to get the bull from Cardinal Campeggio. In June, the Italian cardinal told Cardinal Wolsey that the Pope had prohibited the use of the bull, adding confusingly, 'And no bull.'

In July, Pope Clement (who was being leaned on by Emperor Charles V, if you remember), rescinded the commission to Cardinals Campeggio and Wolsey and the court was formally closed.

We don't know what happened to the bull. It may have ended up in a china shop.

Anne blamed Wolsey for the failure of the process, and whilst Wolsey is focusing on getting that damned bull, Thomas Boleyn and his brother-in-law, Lord Norfolk, are plotting against him. He has made plenty of enemies on his way up the political ladder, and when people see him falling from grace and popularity they jump on the bandwagon. He has fewer and fewer friends. So that doesn't help.

The same is true today in business. If you make enemies on your way up the greasy pole, they will wait to get you when you are on your way down – and accelerate your decline.

Despite the finely worded efforts of Wolsey and his lawyers, and all their scheming, the fact is his enemies were plotting against him. A deliberate leak of information on Wolsey's dealings with Rome, the Emperor and Francis I was made to Anne – or her father – and the distance between the rock and the hard places was getting smaller. When Cardinal Wolsey failed to obtain the divorce from Rome, he was replaced with Sir Thomas More.

In October 1529, Wolsey was deprived of the Chancellorship and required to return the great seal. His number is up and he knows it. He's been nice to everyone he wants something from. And here's the next lesson.

People who are nice to you usually are so because they want something.

Trying to avoid the inevitable, the cardinal gave the king most of his properties and begged him for mercy. In February 1530, King Henry formally pardoned Cardinal Wolsey and confirmed him as Archbishop of York. Anne wasn't happy. Wolsey left London for York two months later to lick his wounds.

He couldn't reach all of them and had to get a servant to do the tricky ones.

However, whilst in Yorkshire he was charged with treason in November 1530. Wolsey pleaded guilty to absolutely anything and everything that the king could think of charging him with, and threw himself at the king's mercy. He died aged 59, at St Mary's Abbey, Leicester, three weeks later on his journey south. Well, if you were charged with treason you'd take your time getting down from Yorkshire to London, wouldn't you?

But it's Henry versus Pope Clement VII that is still the big fight. If Henry hadn't gone at it like a bull in a china shop the story might have ended differently. Maybe that was the message about the bull?

Henry strongly believes that the Pope at the time of his marriage to Katherine, Julius II, had exceeded his powers in going against the statement in the Bible.

But there again, who wrote that?

Who is to say that if a man marries his brother's wife he shall be without children? Is there any evidence to support this? Well, obviously not, but it's in print in the Bible so if you believe in the Bible, it must be true.

For his part, the Pope doesn't want to be seen to be backing off. His cohorts are saying that Henry has no right to force the Pope not only to see things his way but also to accept his own interpretation of canon law. And what we really have here is an old-fashioned ego-driven power struggle. We've seen it nearly 500 years later with the Brexit negotiations...

And maybe if they had got together over a cup of tea it might have all turned out very differently.

Unfortunately, the importing of tea into Britain didn't begin until the 1660s with the marriage of King Charles II to the Portuguese princess, Catherine of Braganza. (Will they ever find a nice English girl like Kate Middleton?) Catherine is thought to have brought tea with her. Certainly Samuel Pepys has him describing drinking 'a china drink of which I had never drunk before.'

Instead of posturing through their cohorts, countless lives over the next 500 years might have been saved. Indeed, even the complexion, names and fan base of Britain's biggest football teams might have been very different.

Maybe I would have married Susan Garlick.

Back to the plot.

It would be easy to explain Henry's behaviour by saying that he is in love. Passionately in love. He's approaching 40 in 1531 and Anne's in her twenties. His wife isn't interesting any more. He wants a son. And he's willing to do anything. And, because he's a king, he does.

He elevates Anne's father to the rather odd but much-coveted title of Earl of Ormonde, and that makes Anne's brother Viscount Rochford. And shortly after that, with Anne regularly by his side at banquets, Thomas Boleyn replaces the Bishop of Durham as Lord Privy Seal, the fifth-ranking officer of state.

The drive to marry Anne has become not only a power struggle between Henry and the Pope but a campaign for Henry to vindicate his kingship.

He should have learned the lesson that Crosby, Stills, Nash and Young would sing of many years later: 'If you can't be with the one you love honey, love the one you're with' A lesson many men in their forties have learned who have found women in their twenties very attractive but who, when the thrill of the chase and the excitement of a night in the Premier Inn has gone, have had to crawl back with their tails between their legs and face chagrin.

Anne is beginning to enjoy herself and abuse the position she's found herself in at court. She's what my mum used to call 'a right little madam'. And she's set herself up for a fall. Lesson? If you've got it, don't flaunt it. Don't rub people's noses in it. The law of causality will come to find you out; for every action there is an equal and opposite reaction. Or, rather, you reap what you sow.

She didn't live her life by the third Golden Rule.

As the whole issue of the possible divorce dragged on, Henry VIII's mind appears more and more to be focusing on whether a pope can tell a king what he can and cannot do. If both are appointed by God (a moot point in itself), then who is to give in when they disagree? Frustration all round.

And the argument is focused on whether Katherine had consummated her marriage with Arthur. But the dispensation given by the Pope to Katherine and Henry at the time was one to cover against all possible eventualities including, therefore, against the possibility that Katherine had indeed consummated her first marriage. Henry VIII, of course, denied the Pope's right to grant such a dispensation in the first place – the central issue of the whole affair, rather than the question of and not so much the Queen's virginity.

It's a lesson we should all acknowledge.

People look for evidence to support an opinion they have already got.

And they can usually find it.

But very often it's just not right. When Louann Brizendine, founder and director of the University of California, San Francisco's Women's and Teen Girls' Mood and Hormone Clinic, published *The Female Brain* she claimed that women speak an average of 20,000 words per day, nearly three times more than the 7,000 spoken by men.

A fact still quoted by people who assume that it's right. But James Pennebaker, Chair of the Psychology Department at the University of Texas had been collecting data on the topic for a decade before Brizendine got her 15 minutes of fame. And he was able to prove that the sexes are about equal when it comes to a war of words.

Instead, he had people wearing a device he called an EAR (Electronically Activated Recorder). It's a digital recorder that subjects can store in their purses or pockets in a sheath similar to a case for glasses. The EAR samples 30 seconds of ambient noise (including conversations) every 12.5 minutes.

Researchers used this device to collect data on the talking patterns of 400 people in Texas, Arizona and Mexico. And the average number of words spoken by men and women were similar at about 16,000 words a day. He did find that women tend to chat more about other people whereas men chat about cars and beer. But as far as the myth of women being more chatty than men goes, it is, quite simply, not true.

Many people who have been very near to death and then revived report the sensation of walking towards a bright light and see it as a religious vision and confirmation of an afterlife.

Books have been written on the subject, and people who want to believe in the afterlife see it as confirmation that there is something out there for us all when we draw our last breath.

Of course, there may well be something beyond death. But the brainwaves of dying patients always show a surge of electrical activity in the moments before their lives end. According to Lakhmir Chawla, an intensive care doctor at

George Washington University Medical Center, the near-death experiences are caused by a surge of electrical energy released as the brain runs out of oxygen.

As blood flow slows down and oxygen levels fall, the brain cells fire one last electrical impulse. It starts in one part of the brain and spreads in a cascade. It is *this* that gives people the impression of being bathed in bright light and a sense of peace as they start to walk into a light-filled tunnel towards the vision of Jesus or Muhammad or Krishna. Sam Parnia at Southampton University's School of Medicine has interviewed hundreds of people who have had cardiac arrests and been brought back to life. Most of them don't have the bright light experience. So if it is a sign of the afterlife why do only a minority experience it?

But people who want to believe that when you die you will see a shaft of light and 'the other side' don't want to know about the work of people like Chawla and Parnia.

Incidentally, those people who have had a near-death experience become happier, more altruistic, less afraid of death and less materialistic according to a Dutch study published in 2001 in *The Lancet*. And given people look for evidence to support an opinion they have already got, you shouldn't assume what someone is saying is true. Say, 'What evidence do you have to support that?'

When I left the world of advertising and embarked on what could very loosely be called a career as a professional speaker, I paid to go on all manner of courses to learn from established speakers on negotiation, relationships, sales, persuasion, influence and so on. And it was a consistent source of amazement to me that many speakers quoted a 'stat' that 55% of communication is body language, 38% the tone of voice and 7% the words. And I would always ask 'What's the source?' or 'What evidence do you have to support that?' Invariably the answer would be that it was 'research'.

In my view that's not good enough. For example, the 55/38/7 figure *did* come from a piece of research. But it was back in 1967. And it's just not true. Even the man responsible for it, Albert Mehrabian, said that it was fundamentally flawed and not intended to be used as it now is.

Henry VIII is doing exactly what most people do – he's searching for evidence to support his view; he's looking for books that say a king is omnipotent. And he finds those books, starts reading them and gets from them what he wants. Like a drunk clinging onto a lamp post, he's using the findings for support rather than illumination.

Eventually Henry used parliamentary legislation to end the dependence of the English clergy on Rome and Henry VIII was recognised as 'protector and only supreme head of the church and clergy in England' in 1531. In addition, Parliament passed a law prohibiting appeals to the Pope in matters of marriage.

I spend a lot of time in Northern Ireland – I'm always made to feel very welcome there – but what they refer to as 'the Troubles' are never very far from people's thoughts. Yet the real root of the factions that still exist in that part of the world can be traced back not just to James I proclaiming by Royal Charter that Derry be renamed Londonderry, but to Henry VIII's motives back in the 16th century. And perhaps if there was a more complete understanding of the original reasons behind the fighting, it might help.

Either way, Henry took Anne off to Dover in October 1532, together with an entourage of twenty-plus ladies including her Aunty Dot and Lady Wallop. They all boarded the ship *The Swallow* and, ten years after she'd left it, Anne found herself back in Calais. 'It's not pretty but at least we can get some cheap booze,' she was overheard to say. However, Calais, at this time, was still part of England, so there was a bit of explaining to do going through Customs and Excise on her return.

It seems likely that this is the point at which Henry at last sleeps with Anne. There was definitely a lot of movement in their cabin but that could have been the rough sea crossing. For ten days Anne acted the role of queen and for his part, Henry is living like, well, a king. They had a wedding ceremony of sorts in January 1533 and, bingo, she's pregnant.

William Warham, the Archbishop of Canterbury, had died in August 1532. Henry needed the holder of that office to annul his marriage (rather than be seen to be doing it himself) so rather conveniently appointed Thomas Cranmer; his own man. By March 1533 Cranmer was consecrated and instituted at Canterbury with the assistance of confirmatory papal bulls. (Not the pot kind; this is more of a formal proclamation issued by the Pope and sealed with a leaden *bulla*.) And Cranmer proceeded to do what was expected of him. As Archbishop of Canterbury he declared the king's marriage to Katherine of Aragon void from the beginning, and pronounced the marriage to Anne Boleyn valid.

On June 1st 1533 she was crowned queen.

Needless to say, Pope Clement VII excommunicated Henry.

It's called 'a rigged deck' nowadays.

It's also called 'burning your bridges'.

And the repercussions would last for hundreds of years.

So, all's well apart from the fact that there are three people in the marriage. Henry, Anne and Katherine. And as Diana, Princess of Wales, was to also find out over 400 years later, when there are three people in a marriage it's not easy...

Following the breach with Rome, Henry VIII, Thomases Cranmer and Cromwell undertook a reorganisation of the church and state.

Cromwell was an interesting guy. For some 14 years he was a solicitor for Wolsey but saved himself from the car crash that was Wolsey's demise by changing horses so fast you couldn't see his feet move. In November 1534 the Act of Supremacy acknowledged that the king 'justly and rightly is and ought to be the Supreme Head of the Church in England'. Henry formally assumed the new title in early 1535.

It was to prove to be a particularly bloody summer. During June and July, the Bishop of Rochester and Sir Thomas More, the king's former chancellor, were convicted of high treason against the king and sentenced to be drawn, hanged, disembowelled, their bowels burned before them and then, just in case they were still wriggling, beheaded and quartered. And, to make double sure, the various body parts to be strewn 'in such places as the king should assign'. The treason was denying that the king was Supreme Head of the Church in England.

It created what is now known as a 'PR issue' for Henry. In the next five years Parliament passed a series of laws aimed at the dissolution of the monasteries and reformation of the Church in England in the direction of Protestantism.

And they didn't just 'dissolve' the monasteries. All monastic houses became state property after Henry VIII pronounced himself Head of the Church in England. They had realised what an excellent source of wealth the monasteries could be.

It's called 'theft' nowadays.

Anne had produced her daughter in September 1533.

If the baby girl, christened Elizabeth and destined to be queen, had been a boy, the face of English history would have been different.

On such things does history turn.

In 1534 the Act of Supremacy had set them up for a happy life, and in 1535 the Archbishop of Canterbury agreed that Henry and Katherine are divorced.

Twenty-six years after they were married.

That summer, whilst the beheadings were going on – or rather, coming off – Henry spent most the time on a progress to the Severn and then across to Hampshire in September. The sport was good – in particular the hawking. Anne accompanied him throughout the trip and by the time they returned to Windsor in October she was pregnant again.

They had called at Wolf Hall in Wiltshire on the way home and had stayed as guests of Sir John Seymour and Margery Wentworth. The eldest of their eight children, Jane Seymour, was lady-in-waiting to Anne Boleyn, having previously been in the service of Mary Tudor, Henry's sister, and also Katherine of Aragon. And Jane's about to play a part in the drama.

At the end of 1535, with Henry having fallen out with Rome, the French refusing to co-operate and acknowledge Anne as queen, no son and heir, and a lot of unhappy English Catholics, it's no longer the Cardinal who is between a rock and a number of hard places. It's Henry – and it's *his* reach that seems to have exceeded his grasp.

On January 7th 1536 Katherine of Aragon died at Kimbolton Castle after a short illness. As far as Anne Boleyn and her family are concerned, all it needs now is for Mary to go the same way as her mother and all their worries are over. She and Henry have a 16-month-old daughter and she is pregnant with what will hopefully be a healthy son and heir. They celebrate the news of Katherine's death the following Sunday by wearing bright yellow from tip to toe. They must have looked like a couple of bananas.

Pride cometh...

Anne miscarried a boy on January 29th and there were 'signs of deformity and abnormality' according to a report by the Spanish Imperial Ambassador to England, Chapuys. There is little or no real evidence to support this. However, just like everyone else at court, Chapuys has his favourites, his agenda and, of course, his self-interest and self-preservation in mind. He was one of Katherine's and Princess Mary's closest allies and despised Anne. And Anne, being Anne Boleyn, returned the feeling.

Chapuys had confidently predicted Anne's fall for several years. He can see the king's shift from Anne to Jane, and it suits the king for there to be a deformity. Henry began to believe that Anne would never give him the healthy son he craved.

We don't really know to what extent Anne fell out of favour because she couldn't produce a son or because Henry fell in love with Jane, but the expression 'whirlwind romance' is probably apt.

Anne has made plenty of enemies. Even her father is about to distance himself from her. And she is now beginning to learn the effect of ignoring the third Golden Rule; you reap what you sow.

Early in 1536 Cromwell discreetly suggests to Jane Seymour's brother, Edward, that he and his wife move to Cromwell's rooms, which are connected through a secret passage to the king's apartments that will allow Henry private – and secret – access to Jane whenever she happens to be visiting her brother.

Which she then did on a regular basis.

Cromwell knows which side his bread is buttered on.

But here's the next lesson. If you are in a secret relationship, you probably shouldn't be in it.

When it comes to going after what you love in life, you shouldn't take no for an answer too easily. But sometimes it's best for everyone that you do.

But before the end of May 1536 Anne Boleyn has been executed on charges of adultery. Yes, that's right. Henry spends six years fighting with Rome as to whether or not he can get divorced, but just over three years after marrying her, Anne is dead and buried. And Katherine too.

What went wrong? To spend so much effort to get your own way and then cast aside the very thing you fought so hard for...

What did happen in the spring of 1536 and what can we learn from it?

Time to learn about the musician, the brother and the bottom wiper in Chapter 6.

The Musician, the Brother and the Bottom Wiper

Born in 1508 and therefore 28 to Henry's 45 in 1536, Jane Seymour could only just about read and write her own name. Not what you would call a scholar. She worked for Queen Katherine, and served Anne Boleyn when she became queen. The first report of Henry VIII's interest in Jane Seymour was in February 1536. She was pale and blonde, the opposite of Anne Boleyn's dark hair and olive skin.

And so the factions begin all over again. As in businesses, once factions begin, the main protagonists *want* people to take sides. And people close *do* take sides and seek favour so that if they've backed the right horse they will ultimately be rewarded.

Anne has seen Henry get rid of one wife and, unless she produces a male heir, she knows he can do it again. 'Am I not a man as other men are?' Henry allegedly says. His ego is getting in the way again and he can't face the fact that he might be the one to blame for the lack of a son. Henry is looking for a reason to rid himself of Anne and, if you look hard enough for it and have enough lackies, you can soon put a case together.

And that's what Cromwell does. Anne's brother's wife is willing to testify that her husband and Anne have been inappropriately intimate, and once the people at court realise that the king has decided that Anne is to go, they start shifting horses too. Anne is on her way out with no way back. She's arrested on the grounds of adultery with her brother and others. And, of course, the king needs the most senior people in the church to find a way to annul his marriage.

Just as Jeffrey Skilling needed Arthur Andersen to give credence and credibility to Enron's scandalous activities. As the service provider – Arthur Andersen – you take the king's shilling if you do as he bids. Bonuses all round. And if you resist and go with your conscience you are left in the waste lands. Over the years it happens.

Again and again.

Arguably the surest sign that a major corporation is headed for trouble is when management experts and professors of business at universities start touting that corporation as a model for every other company to follow.

As they did with Enron.

When Enron spectacularly collapsed in 2001 it was then the biggest bankruptcy in corporate history. It ripped open the catastrophic fault line of unchecked economic avarice, incompetence, selfishness, lies and greed that ultimately led to the meltdowns of Bear Stearns, Lehman Brothers, HBOS, RBS, Northern Rock, Icelandic banks and countless others. Enron had taken just 16 years to grow to assets of $70 billion and 24 days to go bankrupt. A company praised by many pundits as a new business model that met and exceeded its targets, and was used in universities as a model for others to emulate was, with the benefit of hindsight, a house of cards built over a pool of petrol with a lighted match nearby.

And it's not just avarice that causes a fall.

It was 1973 when Paul Simon sang 'Mama, don't take my Kodachrome away'. Thirty-six years later Kodak finally did it. The Eastman Kodak Company took Kodachrome off the market after a run of 74 years. It was, of course, yet another victim of the digital revolution. It had captured some of the most famous wildlife imagery; and, indeed, Abraham Zapruder's 8mm reel of President John Kennedy's 1963 assassination was shot on Kodachrome. To be fair, it's difficult to think of anything else that was invented in 1935 that is still being used today. But it went the same way as videotape, Sony Walkmans and CDs.

Of the biggest top 100 companies in the world when *Titanic* set sail in 1912, less than 20% are still in the top 100 companies in the world today.

When *Titanic* left Southampton there were more than 500 steelworks in Britain. Now more people work in Indian restaurants in Britain than work in the steel industry.

It's a big lesson for anyone in business. You have to keep up with change.

Enron was once hailed as 'America's most innovative company', almost up to the point it was exposed as a glorified Ponzi scheme. Enron made its reputation through complex financial transactions that turned out to be a disguise for massive fraud. As is often the case with companies that fail, it is their own corporate philosophies which contain the seeds of their destruction. The more anyone goes for swift global expansion, the more difficult quality control becomes.

In my home town of Harrogate, Bettys is held up as an icon of how a business should be run. It consistently wins awards for its products, its service and also for being a great employer. It's no coincidence that Bettys will only open up where it can deliver fresh product from its own bakery each day. Similarly, Booths supermarkets in the North West has continued to do very well against the major supermarkets because it has grown steadily, prudently and not gone for swift global expansion.

The people who run those two companies truly care about their company, their customers and their staff. They live their lives by the seven Golden Rules.

And it shows.

Back in 1536, Queen Anne, of course, denies the charges that she has been 'inappropriately intimate' with her brother and others, but the king has his way.

At the end of a long weekend contemplating the future, on Easter Tuesday, April 19th 1536, Henry has convinced himself that he needs to make a change. Anne Boleyn has to be found guilty of something – witchcraft, treason, adultery, whatever. In fact, Henry's brief seems to be to make it up if necessary.

And make it up they do.

The Boleyn family's fortunes are about to change.

And change fast.

It's worth following the chronology of the events of April and May 1536. The Tower of London was a busy place for a few weeks that spring.

23 April: George Boleyn finds he isn't to receive the Order of the Garter, whilst Nicholas Carew – hostile to the Boleyns and one of the court conservatives – does receive the honour.

27 April: Writs go out to summon Parliament – even though it had only been dismissed on the 14th.

29 April: Jane Seymour is given a purse of gold sovereigns and a royal letter whilst she is at Greenwich with Anne. And she refuses to open them. She kisses the letter and hands it back to the delivery boy unopened. We all want what we can't have. Henry is hooked.

30 April: Sir Henry Norris is the first of the 'Philandering Three' to be arrested. He was Groom of the Stool. Basically he had the job of wiping the monarch's bottom after a bowel movement. He's one of those accused of adultery with Anne. He's in the doo-doo in more ways than one. On the same day, the musician Mark Smeaton is arrested and taken to Cromwell's house in Stepney. Questioned, tortured and working out he's probably plucked his last string, he soon confesses to 'violating the queen' three times.

1 May: Anne attends the May Day tournament at Greenwich with her husband. By all accounts Henry was out of sorts and bad-tempered, and he left in the middle of the event. Well, if a week is a long time in politics then the fortnight from Easter Monday to May Day must have seemed like a lifetime.

Anne would never see Henry again.

2 May: Henry tries to get Norris to confess to charges of adultery and, pleading his innocence, Norris is escorted to the Tower.. Never mind the evidence – or lack of it – down you go. And leave the backside cloth for the next man when you leave.

On the same day Anne is arrested by her Uncle, Thomas Howard, Sir William Fitzwilliam and William Paulet on the grounds of adultery with the musician, the brother (George Boleyn) and the bottom wiper.

12 May: Norris and Smeaton – along with Sir Francis Weston and William Brereton are tried at Westminster Hall and found guilty.

15 May: Anne and her brother are tried in the King's Hall of the Tower of London. Guilty as charged.

Were they guilty? Well, as far as the majority of the charges of adultery and treason are concerned there are huge holes in the evidence. More than half of the specific charges are impossible as either Anne or the man concerned was elsewhere at the time; for example, Anne was accused of soliciting Norris at Westminster on October 6th but she was in Greenwich recovering from childbirth. Fact is, when the charges include the proviso from the prosecution that if we can't find you guilty of committing adultery and treason on the days we specify then we'll assume you did so on 'other days and places before and after' you're doomed.

So why was Anne Boleyn arrested, convicted and ultimately executed if she wasn't guilty? Either Henry VIII quite simply wanted her out of the way to marry Jane Seymour and produce a male heir – Anne's miscarriage of a deformed foetus caused Henry to believe that she would never give him a healthy male heir – or the whole thing was orchestrated by Thomas Cromwell and her other enemies.

Every day, all over Britain, people gather in groups to make decisions. Some big, some small, some important, some fairly trivial. That's the decisions, not the people. The outcome could affect anything from the way a business develops to the route a new trunk road takes. It could create a hundred new jobs or add a hundred to the dole queue. And the really frightening thing is that most executives are happy if they get just 60% of decisions right. Which means they don't much mind if they get almost half the decisions wrong. Not surprisingly, governments and businesses waste billions every year making bad decisions. And often it's because the decision was made by a group.

In many areas of life there's such a thing as safety in numbers. For instance, when confronted by an unruly mob of away fans at a train station or perhaps encountering a pride of lions whilst out on safari. But it doesn't really work when it comes to decision-making, thanks to what leading psychologist Irving Janis rather imaginatively terms 'groupthink'. It's a bit like group sex but a lot less interesting and you get to keep your clothes on. Groupthink happens when you get together a group of people with very similar backgrounds, values and interests.

Like a management board, for instance. People who either like, or at least have a healthy respect for, one another. Because of this, a consensus of opinion usually emerges when deliberating a decision, and any evidence to the contrary is automatically rejected. Sometimes even ridiculed. A slap on the thigh, followed by hilarious, raucous laughter and a knowing look usually does the trick.

I should know – my thighs are red raw.

The bottom line is that individual members don't want to rock the boat because it might damage their personal relationships, or even their careers.

A number of experiments have shown that people are quick to adopt the majority position and, crucially, they ignore all the potential alternatives and all the conflicting evidence. So what do you do about it if you want to make better decisions? Well, it's down to someone to make the group aware of the problems with the consensus view and offer alternatives.

Someone needs to be appointed devil's advocate, with the job of trying to spot holes in the decision-making process. According to another leading psychologist in the field, Amiram Vinokur, a key part of this role is to nurture authentic dissent and mould it into constructive criticism. Because if mistakes are not spotted and dealt with in the meeting, they can be a lot more costly and difficult to put right at a later date. Or to put it another way, if nobody is prepared to 'rock the boat' in the meeting, the boat will almost certainly get rocked later.

Think *Titanic*.

But everyone is frightened of Henry. He is omnipotent. No one is asking him whether it's fair and right that Anne has to go. Maybe she has committed these crimes, maybe she hasn't. But she deserves a fair hearing. But with an all-powerful leader and no one challenging his views, the 'team' are all working towards one goal – Anne's demise.

Anne was condemned and due to die. On May 16th Cranmer heard the first of Anne's confessions; on the 17th her marriage to Henry was annulled – because of Henry's liaison with Mary Boleyn – and Anne's alleged lovers were executed.

Anne had asked if a popular, famous French executioner (there were those people in those days) could chop off her head but the executioner from Calais was delayed until noon and then again until the next day.

It happens.

On May 19th 1536, after a hearty breakfast, the Lieutenant of the Tower came for Anne. She wore a black gown, a red petticoat, an ermine mantle and a gable hood. And why not? Her reputation and her legacy is, like everyone else's, affected by how you show up.

Top tip: No matter how you feel, get up, dress up and show up.

People often ask me what is the most important thing about being a professional speaker, and I answer in all honesty and humility that it is turning up. You owe it to the people who have faith in you. When people have booked you the thing that worries them on the day is what will happen if you don't turn up. So I endeavour to arrive earlier than I said I would.

Which is nice for them.

Apparently Anne looked behind her quite a bit – perhaps worried the executioner might strike whilst she wasn't looking. Well, you would, wouldn't you?

She made her speech and knelt before the block. To make sure she looked in the right direction, the executioner called to a member of the audience, 'Bring me the sword.' Anne turned her head, and the executioner struck; the 'Sword of

Calais' had been hidden in the straw. Trick of the trade, I suppose. That's what you pay professionals for. To know what to do and how to do it when the pressure's on. It's nice being good in the kickabout; it's what you do when you're on the pitch playing for real that you get paid for – and that's what separates the men from the boys.

Anne was quietly buried in the Chapel of St Peter ad Vincula inside the Tower of London. Three years and thirty-seven days after she had first dined abroad as queen in 1533.

Anne of just slightly more than a thousand days.

On May 20th 1536, the day after Anne's execution, with Anne's marriage – the 'Great Matter' that Henry fought so hard for – having been made null and void, her daughter, Elizabeth, is declared illegitimate. So is Mary; Henry's daughter from his marriage to Katherine. The very day after Anne loses her life, Henry became betrothed to Jane Seymour and by the end of May, Henry has his third wife.

On July 20th 1536, Henry received the devastating news that his illegitimate son, Henry Fitzroy, Duke of Richmond, had died at the age of 17.

Let's recap as of the start of the school holidays in July 1536.

Henry's just hit 45. Although he's been a very active man in the past, he's suffered a thigh wound in a jousting accident that year that's become ulcerated. He's been on the throne since 1509; the same year he married his late brother's Spanish wife who was six years older than him.

They have a daughter but he wants a son. He's split the church, caused factions, death and in-fighting amongst many of England's families, married his mistress's sister and they, too, have a daughter. He's rid himself of many of his loyal servants and friends, but the influential religious leader, Thomas Cranmer, has become Archbishop of Canterbury and has been let loose to get Protestantism embedded in England.

Twenty-seven years after coming to the throne, Henry has divorced his wife of 27 years, murdered his second wife, lost his much-loved bastard son, has a three-year-old daughter, Elizabeth, brought up as Protestant, as well as a 20-year-old daughter, Mary, who's a staunch Catholic and has a mind of her own.

He also has a new wife, Jane Seymour. As Jim Croce subsequently wrote, 'Which way are you going, which side will you be on? Will you stand and watch while all the seeds of hate are sown? Will you stand with those who say, let his will be done? One hand on the Bible, one hand on the gun.' Quite prophetic, Jim. You could well have been writing about Miss Seymour in May 1536.

Within 50 years of Henry VII – the Lancastrian, if you remember – marrying the Yorkist Elizabeth in 1486 and ending the Wars of the Roses, his son Henry VIII has managed to create a Catholic versus Protestant wrangle that will last for nearly 500 years and counting.

And for what?

CHAPTER 7

Died, Divorced, Beheaded, Survived

On the evening of Anne's execution Henry had dinner with Jane Seymour at a little restaurant on the Strand.

They did that sort of thing in those days.

He then took his barge up to Hampton Court. By 6 o' clock the next morning Jane had joined him there and, after a good breakfast, they made a formal announcement to anyone who wanted to attend the press conference that they were to be married before the end of the month.

Henry wants a new beginning. Many people do. But his 20-year-old daughter still won't accept him as Head of the Church and there's the small matter of his younger daughter, Elizabeth, too. Still, Henry busied himself whilst at Hampton Court for a week, getting the monogrammed linen changed, swapping the coats of arms and generally ridding the various royal palaces of Anne's presence.

On May 30th 1536 Henry and Jane were married at Whitehall Palace. Jane had seen what had befallen Anne by having too much to say for herself and opted for a submissive, adoring role. What she wanted was a son and to help further her family's ambitions. Her oldest brother, Edward, became Viscount Beauchamp, first Duke of Somerset, and was given land and privileges. His position appeared unassailable. The other older brother, Thomas, was made Lord High Admiral but didn't fair quite so well and resentment crept in. He was still unmarried and he possibly saw himself as a husband to either Princess Mary or Princess Elizabeth.

Their father, Sir John Seymour, was to not only fill his boots and get himself a position at court but to embark on a love affair with Edward's wife.

That's right; his own daughter-in-law. When it was discovered, the marriage was annulled and their children declared bastards. Obviously their legal grandfather might also be their biological father. No way of knowing.

And no, I have not made that up.

There are a number of powerful men who come out of all this with very little credit. But Thomas Boleyn and John Seymour are the main contenders for the worst offenders. We can learn from great things and we can learn from poor legacies, and the lesson for all mothers and fathers nearly 500 years later is this:

Live so that when your children think of fairness, caring and integrity they think of you.

Probably the entire Seymour family had been party to the plot to bring Anne to the scaffold. Fact is, after Jane became queen, her family scaled the social ranks, as was befitting the family of a monarch. And it would be easy to see this new cabal that the Seymour family are creating as simply about power and status. But for them – and for the others who want to join a new, powerful group such as this – it is also to help fulfil a deeper psychological need we all have.

Why do we like to join social groups? Well, it's staring you in the Facebook and WhatsApp. The popularity of social media websites serves to underline a basic need in us all. No, not just to share embarrassing pictures with the rest of the world but, rather, to 'belong'.

In fact, it's one of three basic human needs; the other two being to be loved and to feel important. But what's with this in-built desire to join social groups? In the animal kingdom the reason is easy to understand since it's mostly about survival. That's why wolves hunt in packs, birds fly together for safety, and ants achieve more by working in unison. However, for humans, belonging to a group helps us form a view of our social identity which, in turn, contributes to our sense of who we are.

It wasn't just for the money, status and reduced likelihood of being beheaded that everyone suddenly wanted to be part of the Seymour power base Henry was happy to encourage.

Fifty years ago, a famous study by Tajfel demonstrated how complete strangers stuck together even when they had only the smallest thing in common. In his experiment, a group of boys were gathered together and then told they were to be split into two teams. Despite not knowing each other at all, most favoured being in a team with those immediately around them rather than those furthest away. Better the devil you know, I guess.

It's a bit like meeting your countrymen abroad when on holiday. Walking along the prom of a UK resort, you would happily pass by without saying a word. But in a foreign country you're likely to at least exchange pleasantries when recognising that they're from these shores. Wearing Union Jack shorts helps in this respect.

What's more, a funny thing happens when we join a group. We start to behave just like everyone else and follow the 'group norm'. Even when there's nobody in the group called Norm. One of the most famous experiments showing how easily we conform to unwritten group rules was conducted by Solomon Asch of Rutgers University in New Jersey. He asked participants to sit amongst a group of strangers and judge the length of queues of people that were being formed in front of them.

What he didn't tell them was that all the other people had been instructed to lie when asked which was the longest queue. So the unsuspecting participants were looking at several queues of people and it was obvious which was the longest queue. But all the strangers said a relatively short queue was the longest. And sure enough, 75% of participants denied all the evidence from their own senses and instead conformed to the group view as to which was the longest queue.

A similar experiment run by psychology professor Philip Zimbardo of Stanford University wasn't quite so successful. His idea was to place young men into a simulated prison environment with some assuming the role of prisoners whilst others played the part of guards, complete with riot gear. Despite being a psychologist, he clearly hadn't thought through the consequences of the experiment and the likely long-term effects on the mental health of the participants. After less than a week the experiment had to be scrapped when some of the prisoners were becoming too submissive and some of the guards a little too zealous when administering discipline. Needless to say, the emotional fallout from the experiment outweighed any positive conclusions. In fact, I think some prisoners are still on the roof protesting.

So if you want to join a group and become its leader, the first thing to do is conform. Then, when you feel trust has been gained, it's safe to start to show the way. And if you decide to start a group outside of work, don't forget to invite me. Because just like everyone else, I hate to be left out.

Back to the 16th century...

The Seymours had begun to accumulate enemies and grudges during their rise in royal favour. Sound familiar? John died in December 1536, but his royal daughter did not attend the funeral.

In 1537 Jane became pregnant, and Henry was delighted when she gave birth to the much-wanted son and heir. He was named Edward and christened on October 15th, but Jane was weak after the delivery and died just 12 days after giving birth.

Henry had already been preparing his own tomb at St George's Chapel at Windsor Castle, which was where Jane was buried. In the end, she would be the only one of Henry's six wives to be buried with him. She ensured the king's lasting affection when she gave birth to Edward. The infant prince was the only male Tudor heir of his generation; he had two sisters, and Henry VIII's sisters, Mary and Margaret, had several daughters. With Edward now here, Henry felt confident that the throne would not pass to a woman and the Tudor dynasty would survive.

Little did he know.

To his death, Henry talked of Jane in much more affectionate terms than he ever referred to his other wives. Was it the fact that she was the one who bore his son? Was it love? Or was it that she died prematurely?

Those who are cut off in their prime leave memories that improve with time. For many musicians, death is not a final reckoning – it's the best career move they ever made. Rock and pop stars live life in the fast lane and they are twice as likely to die early than the rest of the population. Eddie Cochrane was 21, Buddy Holly 22, Jim Morrison, Jimi Hendrix, Kurt Cobain and Amy Winehouse were all just 27, Marc Bolan was 29, Sam Cooke 33, Glenn Miller and John Lennon were both 40, Elvis Presley was 42 and Freddie Mercury 45.

Within a week of Michael Jackson's untimely death at 51, five of the top ten albums in the UK were his.

In terms of her legacy, dying at 34 turned out to be a good move for Jane.

Within three years of Jane's death, Henry had turned his thoughts to a wife for political alliance. His last two wives had been chosen from the previous queen's team of ladies-in-waiting. This time he married his fourth wife, Anne of Cleves, to gain a political alliance in Europe. He saw her picture, painted by Holbein, thought she was quite pretty and agreed to the marriage.

He's coming up to 50 and now relies on paintings. A sort of 16th-century Tinder – but takes a lot longer. But just as men who now go on the internet dating sites and then fix to meet the woman of their dreams find, portraits are done to show the ladies' best sides. He was sorely disappointed when they actually met, and after only six months the marriage was annulled on July 9th 1540. I don't know about you, but I think I'd want my money back.

To be fair, he had apparently said to Cromwell on his wedding day, 'My Lord, if it were not to satisfy the world, and my realm, I would not do that I must do this day for none earthly thing.'

His 'gut feel' was that it was the wrong thing to do. I think it is without exception that all the CEOs I know can tell several stories of how they have had a negative gut feeling about a potential employee, but they went with the CV, the view of colleagues and the impressive performance at interview – and rued the day they did.

We all form a view of someone very quickly indeed, and we all use the expression 'I had a gut feeling' when we have a thought or, rather, an intuition. Even when we know someone well, we have an intuition that we can't quite explain that things are not as they appear to be. They lack verisimilitude.

We often have a view or opinion but are unable to rationally account for it. And, more importantly the gut feeling turns out to be right.

So where do gut feelings really come from, and should we trust them? Do we only and exclusively use our brains to assess and decide? Well, Dr Candace Pert (formerly a professor at Georgetown University and a Chief of the National Institute of Mental Health in the USA) discovered that the entire lining of the gastrointestinal tract, from the oesophagus to the large intestine, is lined with cells that contain neuropeptides (once believed to exist only in the brain) and receptors.

When I work with people on their presentation skills, they all tell me that they feel their 'insides have been twisted into knots' before a big speech; they talk of 'butterflies in the tummy' – so there is no doubt the stomach listens carefully to the brain. The connections between the two systems are so tight that scientists often refer to them as one entity: the brain-gut axis.

We also make 'snap' judgements on people. We don't forget the first impression that someone makes on us, but we form that judgement in seconds and without actually thinking. So can thinking that takes place so quickly be at all useful? Growing up, we've always been told that we make better decisions when we take the time to carefully evaluate all the relevant information we can find

'More haste, less speed', 'Look before you leap' and so on. Gut feelings and the kind of thinking that goes on in our subconscious brain when we first meet someone have two remarkable things in common. Firstly, they are not deliberate, conscious decision-making processes that we usually associate with 'normal' thinking and, secondly, people consistently tell me that this kind of thinking produces consistently better results.

So should we listen to our instincts, hunches and even our dreams? Well, according to Dr Candace Pert we could do worse. Next time you are asked to justify your gut feelings, tell them that the entire lining of the gastroin-testinal tract, from the oesophagus to the large intestine, is lined with cells that contain neuropeptides and recep-tors. That should have them doing some 'real' thinking about you.

Back to 1540...

Heads had to roll of course, and it was Cromwell, as the marriage's chief architect, who was accused of high treason and executed in July 1540. There's no record of what the king said to Holbein.

Having tried the portrait route and keen to have a mother for the young prince, King Henry VIII had already turned to the tried and trusted formula of looking around at the various ladies-in-waiting for a new wife, so it was no surprise when he met his fifth wife, Catherine Howard, at the English court where she was a lady-in-waiting to Anne of Cleves.

If you recall, he met Anne Boleyn when she was a lady-in-waiting to Katherine of Aragon and met Jane Seymour when she was lady-in-waiting to Anne Boleyn. Did nobody warn Anne of Cleves or was it all part of a plan? Catherine Howard was Anne Boleyn's cousin. Enough said. People look after themselves.

Only a few days after Anne of Cleves was sent back from whence she came, Henry was married to his fifth wife, Catherine Howard. But soon she was also found guilty of adultery and was executed on February 13th 1542.

She'd lasted 18 months.

And King Henry VIII met his sixth and final wife, Catherine Parr, you've guessed it, at the English court. By all accounts, she didn't love him; her affections were with Sir Thomas Seymour, who she later married. But she was forced into the marriage through duty and obligation, and so the marriage took place on July 12th 1543.

That's four wives in the seven years since the beheading of Anne Boleyn; Catherine narrowly escaped punishment for her religious disputes and survived her spouse. The last four go: died, divorced, beheaded, survived. The jousting accident in 1536 had been a major factor in the king's declining health, and he died in 1547 in London at the age of 55. At his death, King Henry VIII left three children from his first three wives, and they all were to have a turn on the English throne: Edward VI, Mary I and Elizabeth I.

King Henry did all he could to protect his son's health; the infant prince lived in safe seclusion until his father wed Catherine Parr. Henry's last wife became a beloved mother to Edward, and he adopted the zealous Protestantism which she championed. He had also grown close to his half-sister Elizabeth, with whom he shared a household for some years. His older half-sister, Mary, was an equally zealous Catholic; her religion and the vast difference in their ages prevented a close relationship.

Before we move to the next Golden Rule that comes from this period, let's put Henry VIII's life on a different time span to give us a better understanding. If Henry's 55 years had been run in a week whereby he was born very first thing on Monday morning, then he'd have come to the throne very early on Wednesday morning, been married to Katherine of Aragon for all of Wednesday, Thursday and Friday, and the other five marriages, two children and other shenanigans would have happened on Saturday and Sunday.

Edward is to become king before his tenth birthday, but his Seymour uncles thought they should run the country. Sound familiar? They battled with, and ultimately lost, the protectorship to the ambitious John Dudley, Duke of Northumberland.

The story of Henry VIII is echoed in the Great Depression of 1929, the financial crisis of 2009, Gerald Ratner and, of course, *Titanic*. And it summarises the fourth Golden Rule to live a happy and successful life that we will look at in the next chapter.

CHAPTER 8

Henry VIII's Omnipotence, *Titanic* and the Fourth Golden Rule

Having been proclaimed unsinkable, *Titanic* set sail in 1912 – a ship designed to accommodate over 3,500 people that was only required to provide lifeboat accommodation for less than 1,000. It also suffered from a shortage of seamen, although its Parisian café employed several hundred waiters. Not surprisingly, factions and disunity were already much in evidence from the moment it left the dockside. Second Officer David Blair had been looking forward to the inaugural trip but was taken off *Titanic* at the eleventh hour. The chairman at the White Star Line, J. Bruce Ismay, had decided that his friend Henry Wilde, Chief Officer of *Titanic*'s sister ship *Olympic* should be transferred to *Titanic*.

And as I pointed out in Chapter 3, as a consequence, the existing Chief Officer became First Officer and Charles Lightoller – the First Officer – replaced Blair as Second

Officer. Mr Blair was deemed too senior to take up the position of Third Officer and was tasked to another ship. No one will know whether it was a simple mistake or a fit of pique but, giving him the benefit of the doubt, Blair was to suffer perhaps the most catastrophic lapse of memory in history, costing more than 1,500 lives. As the ship set off, he forgot to leave behind a vital key. Without it, his shipmates were unable to open a locker in the crow's nest containing a pair of binoculars for the designated lookout.

The lookout was Fred Fleet. He survived the disaster and later told an official inquiry that with binoculars he would have seen the iceberg sooner. Binoculars were referred to as 'glasses' in those days, and Fleet explained that if he had had glasses, that in itself would have been enough to save the ship from disaster. But because of the disunity caused by Henry Wilde elbowing his way on board, no one was willing to lend the lookout their glasses.

On the night of April 14th 1912, it was the existence of factions, and the creation of disunity from those factions, that brought about the downfall of the biggest ship that had ever been built at that time.

The first Golden Rule is not to lose the lesson when you lose; the second is that we shouldn't become complacent; the third, that you reap what you sow. In this chapter we will look at the the fourth Golden Rule that Henry VIII should have adhered to that would have helped him avoid factions and disunity. It is the key lesson for all groups, families, organisations and businesses in order to avoid factions, disunity and hubris.

THE FOURTH GOLDEN RULE:
ALWAYS HAVE A DEVIL'S ADVOCATE.

Whenever people gather in groups to make decisions, someone needs to challenge the group's view and the leader's conclusions. As we discussed in Chapter 6, if no one is prepared to 'rock the boat' in the meeting, the boat will surely get rocked later. And often there are not enough lifebelts to go round.

As we saw in 1912.

No one was strong enough to stand up to J. Bruce Ismay when he jettisoned the original design for *Titanic* and reduced 48 lifeboats by a staggering 32. And if we go back to the Great Depression we see how omnipotence and the lack of a devil's advocate helped create financial ruin.

Back in 1929 enormous power was wielded by a quartet of central bankers: Emile Moreau of the Banque de France; Hjalmar Schacht of the Reichsbank; Benjamin Strong, the founder governor of the New York Federal Reserve; and Montagu Norman, Governor of the Bank of England. They were the guardians of the financial markets. Their actions determined the economic health of nations. They arguably had a bigger impact on the prosperity of the world than any individual government.

Detached from elected politicians and accountable to nobody but themselves, these were the guys who oversaw the world's descent into economic chaos. And, luckily for them, they did it in an age when there were no Sky News journalists to push a microphone under their nose and demand a soundbite. To be fair to the quartet, they hadn't been dealt the best of hands; there was a huge burden of debt heaped on Germany after World War I in the form of reparations, plus corresponding amounts owed to the US by Britain and France.

But even more worrying, all four made big decisions without anyone being allowed to question their conclusions. The actions taken by Montagu Norman crippled British industry. France took an unfair trading advantage for its exporters; Schacht took a reckless gamble in encouraging overseas lending to Germany; and in the USA, interest rates were kept too low in the late 1920s. Benjamin Strong helped to pump up Wall Street's bubble, but that sucked in precious capital from Europe and the whole thing ended in a devastating crash. The pressures on them were enormous.

Just as they had been on Henry VIII.

Strong was the Alan Greenspan or Jerome Powell of his day, perhaps even more powerful for a period than the aforementioned chairs of the Federal Reserve, in that he [meaning Strong] was not obliged to explain himself to Congress from time to time.

Henry VIII had a succession of lackies in More, Wolsey, Cranmer and Cromwell to name but four. But anyone who truly answered back, anyone who offered an alternative view, was not only dismissed but occasionally also dismembered.

Henry lacked a devil's advocate. He was omnipotent.

It might feel good at the time but omnipotence breeds arrogance and hubris. And it always ends in tears. To be truly happy and successful you need someone to be your devil's advocate.

For years, Green Tree Corporation had been very successful in the consumer loans industry in the US. With a $17 billion portfolio, it was the leading lender for owners of trailer homes. And it made its chairman and chief executive grotesquely rich. At one point he claimed to have the highest CEO salary in America.

From 1991 to 1998 annual sales of trailer homes in the US more than doubled. And to make buying one easily affordable, Green Tree was happy to provide mortgages with terms of up to 30 years.

However, there was a major snag with this policy; a huge problem that should have been obvious from the start but which nobody seemed to care too much about. They were all too busy making money.

A trailer home is not like a real house that appreciates in value over time. It's more like a car that depreciates in value from the moment it's bought. And to compound the problem, most only have a lifespan of 20 years. As they say in the US, 'do the math'. Anybody who did obviously didn't wake up and smell the coffee.

The long-term problem was swept under the carpet and replaced with a short-term rug known as 'affordability'. This was the only thing people saw; the only thing that was sold to them. Why was it allowed to happen?

Because there was no devil's advocate.

And whose fault was that? The people who can't see further than the monthly payment or the guy who in 1995 trousered a base salary of $433,000? (They were big pants.) He also benefited from a whopping cash bonus of $6 million and a stock bonus of $60 million.

At the start of the 21st century, the US Treasury Secretary was forced to stuff billions of taxpayers' dollars into the ailing insurance giant AIG. But no one played devil's advocate and asked the 'What if?' questions. No-one thought to attach conditions to the new funding so that obscene bonus payments were impossible. The lunatics were running the asylum. AIG had got rich in the country's heyday insuring the concrete and steel of American industry, only to destroy itself chasing phantom fortunes at the Wall Street card tables. Like a dissolute king gambling away a country's hard-fought assets.

The bailout came just after AIG had posted the largest quarterly loss in American corporate history – some $61 billion. In the final three months of 2008, the company lost more than $27 million every hour. The problem was that no mechanism had been put in place to search the balance sheets of companies like Enron, AIG and Lehman Brothers. Companies that held life-or-death power over ordinary people.

Who allowed this to happen?

It needed a devil's advocate.

In the case of Enron it was a journalist, Bethany McLean, who was brave enough to ask CEO Jeffrey Skilling how Enron actually made its money. That was in March 2001. *The Wall Street Journal* began to dig but even in October 2001 Chairman Kenneth Lay said there was 'absolutely no accounting issue, no trading issue, no reserve issue'.

What was within the walls of their impressive building in Houston was hubris, greed and downright stupidity. And that created all the infighting.

The very shape of our country and the divisive religious beliefs is not an unfortunate accident. It's down to Henry VIII's greed and stupidity and lack of real concern for others. And the repercussions of his reign are still felt. The economic fiasco that was created by people on Wall Street and in the City of London at the start of this century was down to selfishness, greed, stupidity and the lack of a devil's advocate.

Just as *Titanic* was allowed to set sail with over 2,000 souls on board but only enough lifeboats for less than half.

Edward Liddy of AIG admitted mistakes were made when the company strayed from its core insurance competencies to launch a credit-default-swaps portfolio in 1987. But he makes it sound like a latter-day Oliver begging for more soup; hungry and sick from being left out in someone else's financial weather. The fact is they had spent more than a decade systematically scheming to evade US and international regulators and making colossal, world-sinking $500 billion bets with money they didn't have, in a toxic and completely unregulated derivatives market.

After they wrecked the financial world, they then rather cunningly granted themselves almost unlimited emergency powers to clean up their own mess. And so the leaders of companies like AIG ended up not penniless and in jail, but being helped out by 'our partners in the government' as Liddy rather insouciantly described it.

AIGFP – a London-based subsidiary of the American insurance company – ought to have been regulated by our own Financial Services Authority (FSA). But the Office of Thrift Supervision in the US (OTS), which supervises the industry that offers 'affordable' home financing for Americans, managed to convince us that it had the muscle to regulate its own giant companies. But they didn't. At least, unlike Henry's regulators, no one at the OTS was sent to the scaffold. They concluded there was no big credit risk because they were told there was no big credit risk.

Just like people believed J. Bruce Ismay when he said *Titanic* was unsinkable.

AIG had no one doing the counterbalance checks. When Joe Cassano, the head of AIGFP left the firm, he had led the company into the largest bailout in American financial history. However, they not only allowed him to keep $34 million in bonuses, they kept him on as a consultant on a nice little earner of $1 million a month. After all those years letting him run wild and paying insane bonuses, AIG decided to pay a further $450 million in bonuses to the employees in his old unit, AIGFP. Cassano was an autocratic bully who thought he could do anything. True, he brought many people to their knees, but at least he couldn't send people to the guillotine.

However, for those who lost money, it probably felt like it.

Seventy-five years after the sinking of *Titanic*, Britain suffered its second biggest peacetime maritime disaster when the *Herald of Free Enterprise* capsized on leaving Zeebrugge harbour in Belgium. At first it appeared to be a terrible accident.

But then we learned that the ferry had sailed with the bow doors open. Despite being against regulations, this was common practice to allow vehicle exhaust fumes to clear the deck more quickly. Also, vehicles and lorries had not yet been chained to prevent them from moving. Again, this was against regulations but it ensured the ship left port on time. The capsizing of the *Herald of Free Enterprise* wasn't an accident but rather an accident waiting to happen. One day, in rough seas, water was bound to flood in through the open bow doors. One day, this was bound to cause vehicles to slide to one side and make the ship list dangerously. And one day, it would eventually capsize with a breathtaking loss of life.

That day was March 6th 1987.

A total of 193 passengers and crew died because nobody was willing to play devil's advocate. After a public inquiry, Lord Justice Sheen published a report identifying a 'disease of sloppiness' and negligence at every level of the Townsend-Thoresen's hierarchy. Blame was attributed to the company's management and, in particular, four crew members of the ship.

Hubris.

And in 2012, exactly 100 years after the sinking of *Titanic*, a certain Domnica Cemortan had been dining and flirting with Captain Francisco Schettino on the bridge of the *Costa Concordia* when the huge cruise ship struck rocks off an Italian island. The 52-year-old Schettino may have been trying to impress the 25-year-old Moldovan when his ship sailed off course. Domnica admits that not only had she been alone with Schettino in his cabin earlier during the evening of the tragedy, but that they had shared a passionate kiss, which she suspected was a prelude to them becoming lovers.

Domnica admitted that her luggage had been left in the captain's cabin, but says it was only a temporary arrangement while she waited for a cabin to become available.

Oh yeah?

She said afterwards, 'He once told me that I had both beauty and brains. What woman would not want to hear such words – especially when there were many women much more beautiful than me on board the ship?' The captain invited her to the bridge, 'to see a beautiful panorama of the Giglio island off the Tuscan coast'.

The ship ran aground and 32 people lost their lives. And Schettino deserted the ship. He said he hadn't had his glasses whilst on the bridge and that he 'just kind of fell into the lifeboat'.

Sound familiar?

Why were none of his crew stopping him?

Schettino was sentenced to ten years for manslaughter, five for causing the shipwreck, one for abandoning the ship before passengers and crew were clear, and one month for lying to the authorities afterwards. Costa Crociere, the company that owned the ship, sidestepped potential criminal charges in 2013 by agreeing to pay a €1million fine.

In 2019 a Russian cargo ship, the *Seagrand*, carrying 1,500 tons of steel coils rather comically crashed into the bi-level Gwangan Bridge in Busan on the coast of South Korea. During the time of the crash, the ship was going in the opposite direction to its planned course. Where were the checks? Why was there not a co-captain to play devil's advocate and question decisions?

The echoes of Captain Smith of *Titanic* and Captain Schettino of the *Costa Concordia* are there for all to see.

The captain of the *Seagrand* was arrested. He was found to have a blood alcohol level three times the legal limit.

Hubris personified.

Our next lesson is echoed in the words of a famous Michael Jackson song. If you're going to make a change, you need to start with the man in the mirror. Unless, of course, you're a woman.

Either way, if you want to make the world a better place then take a look at yourself and then make a change.

Take responsibility.

When Adam Applegarth was at the helm at Northern Rock, his Group Financial Director, Bob Bennett, was arguably his devil's advocate; his 'safe pair of hands' to Applegarth's 'energetic, youthful, growth-orientated individual', to quote Bennett. But Bennett retired in 2006 and, in common with many building societies, they ignored repeated warnings from the Financial Services Authority to clean up their books without any censure.

RBS, AIG, Northern Rock, Bear Stearns; the list goes on. To give you an idea of the bailout cost to the taxpayer, imagine if a fund had been set up during the reign of Henry VIII. Every week £1 million of taxpayers' money is paid into it. And then one day, almost 500 years later, it's all handed over to the banks.

That's about the size of it.

So who's to blame?

The individuals who were guilty of greed, hubris and then disunity? Well, that's basic human nature. It's what happened to the Beatles, Gerald Ratner and Marks and Spencer under Rick Greenbury. It is what happened to Manchester United after becoming the first English team to win the European Cup in 1968. They were relegated within six years. The same time it took Henry to have Anne Boleyn beheaded after first wooing her.

It is what happened to Liverpool F. C. after three years of being owned by two guys who despised each other; Tom Hicks and George Gillett. Liverpool failed to qualify for the Champions League for the first time since they had last won it, five years before, and ended up in the courts.

Liverpool F. C. used to have the key component of all successful empires: continuity. They had a sound board-room, a judicious succession of managers steeped in the same great tradition, and a dynasty of players. At the time – for those who have not studied history – it seemed inevitable that Liverpool would carry on for ever. And whilst rivals gloat, they also have to live with the real truth: that all empires decline and fall. Even those that appear unbeatable.

Fact is, everyone is trying to beat you. So you have to work that little bit harder to stay ahead. The people at the top must not be greedy or complacent. Instead they must work together and accept the need to constantly improve. Because when you recognise that change is necessary, you are more likely to make the right changes.

It's easy to say that the people who claim to have foreseen the unholy mess in the financial sector around 2007 and 2008 only crawled out of the woodwork after the bad news became public. But there were those, like Paul Wilmott, one of the world's leading financial mathematicians, who had been warning for years that the models used by banks to value their assets were just plain wrong. Wilmott stood up in front of paying audiences and declared that the formulas were relied on too heavily and that bankers were paid too much. Quite a few people stormed out of his conferences, slamming the door for effect on the way out. He pointed out that following the formulas was like relying on your seatbelt to drive crazily; it might save your life but it won't stop you from crashing. And the FSA can't afford to pay the best people so they aren't strong enough to be the devil's advocate. We need people who are clever enough not only to realise that something is wrong but also understand what it is and be strong enough to say it.

Paul Wilmott was not alone. Niall Ferguson – a professor at Harvard no less – offered his thoughts to the great and good of the rich and self-satisfied bankers in autumn 2006 and was dismissed as an alarmist. The suggestion was even made to the organisers that instead of having an outside speaker they should offer a screening of *Mary Poppins*.

Given that this was suggested by an American, the irony of the film's plot – a run on the bank – was sadly lost.

And how was it that Bernie Madoff was able to pull off one of the biggest Ponzi schemes in history?

The secret life of Bernard Madoff unravelled as he stood in his Upper East Side apartment in a pale blue bathrobe and slippers, facing two FBI agents. 'We're here to find out if there's an innocent explanation,' they told him. 'There is no innocent explanation,' Madoff replied. He was responsible for over $50 billion worth of global losses. In its conception, the scam is a timeless classic. Madoff later confessed to his sons, Mark and Andrew, that his money-management business was 'just one big lie...a giant Ponzi scheme.' Clearly unimpressed, it was his sons who shopped him to the authorities. Madoff managed $17 billion directly for clients but, through derivatives, an estimated $50 billion was banking on his performance. Yet the complex trading he claimed to be carrying out in his closed-off eerie on the 17th floor of the Lipstick Building in mid-town Manhattan was a sham; the magic returns were simply cash brought in from new victims.

The list of Madoff's victims was vast and eclectic. They ranged from charities to such well-known names as Steven Spielberg. The fact that he often turned down would-be punters only boosted his cachet; people spent years trying to get onto his client list. Those he turned down no doubt felt hurt and rejected – but they were the fortunate ones that presumably he liked too much to rip off.

But just as it was with Cassano, Liddy, Ismay, Skilling, Applegarth, Maxwell, Goodwin and Henry VIII (to take just a handful of names from a very big list) there were, with hindsight, plenty of red flags. No one seemed to know what Madoff was doing. Regulators who visited in 2005 and 2007 gave him a clean bill of health – despite reports that the auditors of his massive fund consisted of three people operating out of a 13ft by 8ft office in what the Americans call 'Nowheresville'.

When Madoff described his investment method as 'a split-conversion strategy', no one knew what it meant, but took it as another sign of his investment genius. He could have told them it was a split-personality-double-bluff technique and nobody would have raised an eyebrow. Except maybe Bernie himself, who had eyebrows the size of his ego. Now he is assured of his place in history. As Warren Buffett likes to say, 'It's only when the tide goes out that you learn who has been swimming naked.'

And it would be easy to conclude that this 'crash and burn' we saw in 1929 and the early part of the 21st century is a modern phenomenon, but we can go back as far as the 17th century to see how avarice and a belief that things could go on forever left people in ruins.

In the 1630s the price of tulip bulbs rose spectacularly and, one after the other, the Dutch rushed to the tulip markets like flies around a honey-pot. Everyone imagined that the new-found passion for tulips would last forever and that wealthy people from every part of the world would flock to Holland and pay whatever prices were asked for them. Farmers mortgaged whatever they could to raise cash to begin trading, and tulip mania reached its peak during the winter of 1636–37, when some bulbs were changing hands ten times in a day. A particularly rare Violetten Admirael van Enkhuizen bulb, that was about to split in two, sold for more than ten times the average annual salary at the time. But the tulip market crashed spectacularly and the fall, as usual, was even quicker than the rise.

It's a lesson we still haven't learned nearly 400 years later. If things seem to be too good to be true, they usually *are* too good to be true.

There was no doubt a failing in the regulatory regime in America but the get-rich-quick investors – now renamed 'victims' were also guilty of stupidity, greed and carelessness.

The devil's advocate needs to start at the beginning; they need to imagine the chain of events from scratch and foresee the future, rather than be bound by the paths already trodden. Everyone in business has pursued a debt or two. Sometimes you've pursued it for so long that you feel bound to carry on. Often it takes someone else to point out that you need to let it go. If you want a simple example, think of a time when you spent hours on a PowerPoint presentation. You no doubt spent far too long and ended up with far too many slides. But it's difficult to edit them down – which will always make it much better – simply because you had already spent so much time getting to where you are. And it seems like a waste to throw it all away.

Running your own finances is actually pretty simple. Indeed, running a company's finances is straightforward. Don't spend more money than you can afford to lose; if you're going to have debt, make sure you can pay it back; always have a Plan B and always be ready to tighten your belt if the ride gets rocky. Government debt is not only bad economic policy but also morally unacceptable because it makes your children responsible for paying for what you bought.

Of course, there's a neat irony in that if, like me, you seem to spend most of your money on them in the first place.

However, generally speaking, if you are personally in debt you have no one to blame but yourself. It's your own damn fault. You needed a devil's advocate – a good one.

And you have to listen. My good friend Gerald Ratner had a devil's advocate. She was called Lynne Franks. She strongly recommended that he didn't refer to his own product as 'crap'. She strongly recommended that he didn't suggest an M&S prawn sandwich would last longer than a pair of his earrings. But he didn't listen. J. Bruce Ismay was strongly advised to use 'Best Best' rivets on the bow of *Titanic*. But they used a grade down from the best-quality iron, known as No 3, graded simply 'Best'.

Grade 3 rivets have higher levels of slag and are more likely to splinter when put under intense pressure. *Titanic* was designed to stay afloat if up to four of its sealed compartments were flooded. However, pretty soon rivets were popping faster than the buttons on Boris Johnson's shirt after a blowout at the Chinese. And so a fifth and fatal compartment flooded, condemning the vessel to the depths.

Ismay was advised against having only 16 lifeboats on a ship that would travel on its maiden voyage with over 2,000 souls on board.

But he didn't listen.

It's an established fact that *Titanic* had had a coal fire in the three-storey-high coal bunker on the ship for days before she sailed. During the inquiry after the sinking, Crewman Charles Hendrickson was brought up to testify and talked about the fire. He explained the fire was known of before *Titanic* left Belfast. He and three or four other men worked to put out the fire, but the only way to put out a coal fire in a bunker like this was to put the burning coal into the ship's furnace.

Further testimony from the lead stoker of *Titanic* – Fred Barrett – shows how extensive the fire was and that the bulkhead by the coal area was significantly damaged by the fire. Movement of the metal and buckling – in the area the iceberg hit – was reported, but nothing was done to address the damage.

Because the focus of J. Bruce Ismay and Captain Smith was on getting to New York in record time.

Simon Cowell is one of the most successful television and music executives the world has ever seen. And he recognises the need for the devil's advocate. In the boot camps, he insists on each judge having a sounding board. Including himself. On all his TV shows he is not the only judge.

The first devil's advocate (the *advocatus diaboli*) was appointed by Pope Leo X in the early 16th century; his duty was to prepare in writing all possible arguments, even at times seemingly slight, against the raising of anyone to the honours of the altar. The church's aim was to prevent anyone from receiving those honours who were not worthy. In a nutshell, to list everything unfavourable about the candidate. Sixtus V formally established the office in 1587 and the office was abolished in 1979 by Pope John Paul II.

Why did he abolish it?

It's just as relevant today as it's ever been.

CHAPTER 9

Teddy's Uncles, the Nine-Day Queen and the Fifth Golden Rule

People often ask me the secret of good time management and I always reply with the same words. 'Ask me another time when I'm not running late.'

Only kidding.

Good time management lies in the ability to distinguish between the important and the urgent. For instance a leaking roof requires urgent attention, whilst it's merely important to fix a loose roof tile.

Once you've made the distinction, you then need to allocate time to do the important things. That's the 'secret' of good time management. If you fail to allocate time for things that are important but not urgent, then one of two things usually happens. Either the roof eventually leaks and the problem becomes urgent or the roof doesn't leak and the problem doesn't get fixed at all. And, of course, if you wait until something becomes urgent, it's usually more difficult and costly to fix.

There are exceptions, of course. The website lastminute. com can offer some great deals if you put off your decision to the last minute. But the trade-off is that you might not get exactly what you want. And, in life, we usually know what we want. My wife is still fuming about that sky-diving package I bought her. It was an absolute bargain.

Once things become important and urgent they have to be done in a hurry. But when you allocate time for things that are important but not urgent you are forward planning.

So fix your roof when the sun is shining. Creosote that fence before the bad weather comes. Pack your suitcase before leaving home. I know that last one doesn't quite fit but I was struggling for a third and it's still reasonably sound advice.

But what if you fail to allocate time and things don't get done at all? You never do get to see Naples or take that African safari. Those salsa lessons you promised yourself are now a distant dream thanks to your arthritic hip. And imagine if your family never has the pleasure of hearing you play the tuba. Actually, that's probably a good thing.

If you don't allocate time for things that are important but not urgent then you run the risk of never doing them at all. And you may live the rest of your life with regret. Particularly when you get towards the end and can no longer do what was once important but not urgent.

However, distinguishing between things that are important but not urgent is only one part of the task. You also need to be able to prioritise what you do. The best way is often by writing them down in a list. People often complain that they have so much to do, they don't know where to start. Well, if you write a list, you will know exactly where to start.

At the top.

As you may have experienced, airlines are fond of creating priority services to attract extra revenue. For instance, you can take advantage of priority check-in and priority boarding. You don't take off any sooner, you just get to sit in your seat for longer. And, of course, in the event of an emergency, it's women, children and motivational speakers first.

Well, someone's got to cheer up everyone in the lifeboats.

It's important to distinguish the urgent things from the important things, and also prioritise how you deal with them. So do that business planning. Fix that meeting with a key potential customer. Make that call that is important but not urgent.

If you are calling an existing client you may well find that complacency has settled into the relationship and that the call can unearth a problem that can be nipped in the bud.

Fix the roof and paint the fence. Spend more time with those closest to you, unless it happens to be a stalker – when you should walk more quickly and try not to panic. Enjoy your time with elderly parents or grandchildren before it's too late. Above all, have fun. It's important that you do, even though it often doesn't seem the most urgent thing.

As I say, if you don't allocate time for things that are important but not urgent, one of two things happens. Most often they become important *and* urgent AND DON'T GET DONE AS WELL.

We aren't here long. Fun is underrated and undervalued. Most people don't see the real value of having fun with friends, the importance and joy of developing loving relationships and making a positive contribution. It's easy to decry the arts – and in particular comedy – as irrelevant but it is to miss the point. What is the purpose of it all if we don't have any fun?

Life is short. You should enjoy it. Don't make things serious that don't have to be.

Of course we have to do things that are important and urgent. In business, that often involves doing things that are necessary to make money, keep the company afloat, do deals, etc. But often the firefighting aspect of doing things that are important and urgent (and it's often the pyromaniacs who like firefighting the most) is that these things are not done as well as they might have been if they had been done when they were important but not urgent. Because most things that are important and urgent started in the quadrant of important but not urgent.

We spend too much time doing things that are not important and not urgent. We spend too much time doing things that are urgent and *seem* to be important. Often they're important to someone else.

And so we live our 4,000 weeks or so without allocating enough time to having fun with our children. And whilst some people do leave a legacy in business, literature and the arts, most people's legacy is quite simply their children.

Allocating time for things that are important but not urgent means that not only do you plan your time better, plan your fun and plan your holidays, but also you plan your own career better. I meet too many people who started life as a plasterer when they were aged 16 or started working for a car hire company when they were 17 and they are still doing that 50 years later.

And wished they had made different decisions many years ago. And rightly or wrongly they now feel it's too late to change.

If they've enjoyed doing whatever it is they do and fulfilled their potential that's absolutely fine. Indeed, the man who told me that he had the best job in the world – and was extremely happy as a result – was a man who ran a stretch of canal in the north of England for British Waterways. Not everyone's cup of tea, but it was *his*. Unfortunately, I meet too many people in their fifties who are just waiting for retirement in their sixties. And all that came about because they didn't know the fifth Golden Rule; you have to allocate time for things that are important but not urgent.

THE FIFTH GOLDEN RULE:

ALLOCATE TIME FOR THINGS THAT ARE IMPORTANT BUT NOT URGENT

What Edward VI seemed to spend most of his six short years on the throne doing were things that were important for other people but not for him or his subjects.

Let's recap.

The son of Henry VIII, Edward had been born in October 1537 at Greenwich Palace in London and his mother, Jane Seymour, had died 12 days later. On the death of his father in January 1547, he became Edward VI at an age when most youngsters have not finished junior school. Henry had already appointed Edward's uncle, Edward Seymour, to serve as Lord Protector of the Realm and Governor of the King's Person whilst the young king was playing out like kids should, but the nine year old himself had always preferred his more flamboyant uncle, Thomas Seymour, the Lord High Admiral. They were both brothers of his late mother and there was no brotherly love lost between them.

Thomas decided to bet. And lost.

He plotted against his brother, Edward, and was executed within two years of Edward VI coming to the throne – in March 1549.

Uncle Edward Seymour (the Duke of Somerset) was, in turn, deposed by John Dudley, first Earl of Warwick, and executed in January 1552. Henry VIII had appointed a well-balanced council but as the opinion of the members of the council changed, the plans of Henry VIII suffered. Uncle Edward had some strong opinions and practically ruled England from 1547 to 1549. It was he who declared war against Scotland as they refused the marriage proposal of Edward (that's him, not his nephew, the young king) with Mary of Scotland. Mary was married to the French prince, resulting in poor relations between England and Scotland.

You are forgiven if you have a sense of déjà vu here. We have a young boy as king, two uncles squabbling for power and a political schemer in the mould of Wolsey and Cromwell in John Dudley. Relations between England and Scotland aren't too clever either.

Familiar?

John Dudley was 35 when young Edward VI came to the throne and his father, Edmund Dudley, had been Henry VII's finance minister. Despite the fact that Edmund had been found guilty of 'constructive treason' in 1509 and executed in 1510, the Dudley family had managed to hang on in there and John Dudley had made a name for himself fighting the Scots in 1544 and the French in 1545. Dudley was a Protestant and formed a convenient partnership with Edward Seymour against the Catholic Duke of Norfolk.

In spite of a portrait of Edward as a vivacious two year old he was a frail child and a short life was anticipated for him from his early years.

That didn't prevent him benefiting from a good education but that, in turn, only taught him to conjugate some Latin verbs and read a bit of Aristotle's *Ethics*. No match for Dudley and his pals high on self-interest. Interestingly, he recorded with apparently cold-blooded indifference the execution of both his uncles, and he certainly made no attempt to mitigate the harassment of his Catholic sister, Mary.

Fact is, young Edward had been so impregnated with the divine right of kings and the divine truth of Protestantism that he thought he was entitled and bound to override the succession as established by law and exclude a Catholic from the throne. His last recorded words were vehement injunctions to Thomas Cranmer to sign the will. He was brought up believing he was special and could live by special rules and get away with anything.

Bit like Jose Mourinho really.

When he was crowned there were no less than three crowns placed on his nine-year-old head. Cranmer emphasised to the young boy at the coronation that no one had the right to hold him to account. He was answerable only to God. The implications of the absolutism established by Henry VIII were now there to be seen.

As a child he wrote that the Pope was 'a bad man; the true son of the Devil'.

When someone believes they are omnipotent it always ends in tears.

Bit like Jose Mourinho really.

Edward himself was by all accounts a decent young man. Despite not being allowed to run the country as such, he was responsible for introducing a uniform Protestant service in England based on his *Book of Common Prayer* in 1549.

He was 11 years old.

Marriage vows in the form 'to have and to hold from this day forward, for better for worse, for richer for poorer, in sickness and in health, to love and to cherish, till death us do part' have been recited at UK church weddings since the publication of Edward's efforts.

His father had amended the rules to marry several times; Edward never married himself but the wedding service that we are all so familiar with in Britain now was written by these two individuals.

Henry VIII didn't really have a religious policy, beyond demanding that the clergy were obedient to him rather than the Pope. He was a greedy, cynical, tyrannical, providential egomaniac who happened to lay the foundations of our modern religious and political tradition. His son merely carried on his good work, and Edward VI's legacy is there for all to see and hear whenever you attend a marriage in a British church.

Looking back, he rushed the *Book of Common Prayer*, written mainly by Cranmer but credited to the boy king. It was important – to him at any rate – but he thought it was urgent and he should have taken more time to fully think through the implications of such a book.

The *Book of Common Prayer* was the book to which all English people must pray and live by. The book was Edward's attempt at finishing off Catholicism in England.

At a family Christmas party in 1550 with Edward and his two sisters together, a family quarrel developed.

It happens.

The 13-year-old Edward upbraided his 34-year-old sister Mary about her continued devotion to the Catholic religion and daring to break his laws and take Mass. But Mary was having none of it. When she was next summoned to court a few weeks later, she went with all her cohorts carrying rosaries to hammer home the point she was Catholic. And she had a trump card. Unless Edward allowed her to practise Catholicism she would ask her Spanish cousin, the Holy Roman Emperor, Charles V, to declare war on England.

Bet that's not happened at any Christmas family squabble you've been involved in.

Edward backed down and as it became apparent he would not live long, the issue of succession became a major issue. He needed a male, Protestant relative he liked, and his sister didn't fit any of the criteria.

But Mary was, after all, the rightful heir to the throne.

And time was not on his side. Edward's potential would never be realised.

In 1549 Dudley was appointed Lord Admiral. In 1550 he became Grand Master of the Household. In 1551 he became the Duke of Northumberland and also Earl Marshal of England. That was the year Edward Seymour was executed for conspiracy. Then Dudley increased his wealth by taking a great deal of church land.

Shocking.

Many years later Desmond Tutu said 'When the missionaries came to Africa they had the Bible and we had the land. They said "Let us pray." We closed our eyes. When we opened them we had the Bible and they had the land.'

Equally shocking.

Perhaps a little too ambitiously, John Dudley arranged for the marriage of his fourth son, Guildford Dudley to Henry VII's great-grand daughter, Lady Jane Grey. And Dudley then persuaded the sickly, 14-year-old Edward to name Lady Jane Grey as his heir. Dudley saw it as important AND urgent.

With Dudley almost certainly standing over him and playing the religious card, the king to handwrite a document on June 21st 1553 that excluded both Mary and Elizabeth from succeeding to the throne on account of their illegitimacy and expressed his wish that his successor should be Lady Jane Grey.

In his schoolboy handwriting the document he wrote, entitled 'My device for the succession', still exists.

And with Edward's signature at the bottom, that meant that John Dudley's 17-year-old son would be king.

The expansion in Dudley's influence and potential wealth had this happened is difficult to estimate – but politically he would have been all but untouchable. However, there was one major weakness in this plan – it had to work. If it failed, the consequences for anyone associated with it were obvious. If it wasn't to be Lady Jane Grey then there's quite a queue. In addition to Edward's half-sisters, Mary and Elizabeth, there was also Edward's aunt, Lady Frances Brandon, who was the daughter of King Henry's younger sister, Mary, by Charles Brandon.

Looking back it was a very high-risk strategy for the Protestant John Dudley. Having been effectively running the country whilst Edward was alive, if his plot to get Jane Grey to be queen failed it would result in facing the worst of what the staunchly Catholic Mary would throw at him.

And before the end of the summer of 1553, throw she would.

There's a lesson that Dudley didn't learn and that all gamblers need to learn. Don't bet more than you can afford to lose. Especially on a game where you don't know all the rules.

Dudley had not bargained for the instinctive reaction of the people to support the person who they saw as being the legitimate heir to the throne: Mary. As we will see, she fled to East Anglia – the region where Dudley had ruthlessly put down a rebellion. It was an area where there was little support for the man who had done nothing to help the rural poor and where most were conservative and would have had an instinctive loyalty to the daughter of Henry VIII. Having 'lost' Mary, Dudley's supporters in London started to abandon him and he became a very isolated figure.

And there's another lesson from Dudley for anyone who wants to be a leader: we don't want someone we agree with all the time, but we do want someone we trust all the time.

It is rumoured that Dudley cruelly prolonged the illness of Edward, who was in excruciating pain, in order to prepare for the succession of Lady Jane Grey. The king eventually died an agonising death on July 6th 1553 at Greenwich Palace when only 15, possibly from a combination of tuberculosis (consumption) and the measles. He, like his half-sister Mary, had congenital syphilis from his father, Henry VIII, and his condition was complicated by consumption.

Henry's children had reaped what he had sown well after his death.

Such was the sensitivity of Dudley's scheme that he managed to keep Edward's death secret from most people for three days. In this time he put into being the plan that he had been so careful to construct. Lady Jane Grey, the Protestant 15-year-old great-grand-daughter of Henry VII – who most likely never really wanted to be queen – was actually proclaimed queen of England four days after Edward's death.

Who by? Well, er, John Dudley.

He really was deceiving himself at this point.

Apparently, 94% of university professors believe they are better at their job than their colleagues. Most people think they are better than average. You probably do too. And, by definition, that must mean that most people think they are better than most. The question is, does it matter? Is self-deception a good or bad thing in the workplace?

Americans George Quattrone and Amos Tversky conducted a classic social psychology experiment to study self-deception. As is often the case in such experiments, the researchers lied to the participants about every aspect of the study. Firstly, they told them the study was about the 'psychological and medical aspects of athletics'. Then they tricked them into believing that a measure of good health could be gauged by the length of time you could submerge your arms in very cold water.

Naturally, this was nonsense. All it showed was how ready they were to deceive themselves and what they would do for $50. Typically, most people could endure the cold water for about 30 seconds. To make participants believe the study was real they were given other tasks to do as well. Walking over hot coals with no shoes on wasn't one of them but it would have made an interesting footnote. Instead, they did a stint on an exercise bike.

Crucially, they were then given a short lecture about how life expectancy depended on your type of heart. Lying through their teeth, and presumably just managing to suppress a giggle, the researchers revealed that there were two types of heart: one associated with poor health and one associated with top-class athletes.

Continuing with the porkies, the researchers then said it was possible to tell which type of heart you had by measuring your tolerance to cold water *after* exercise. They'd just worked up a sweat on the bikes, remember. But here's the rub. One half were told that an *increased* tolerance to cold water indicated a strong heart, whilst the other half were told that it was a *decreased* tolerance to cold water.

You can probably guess the outcome. Everybody deceived themselves into believing that they had an athlete's heart by either enduring the cold water for less or more time than previously – depending upon the lie they were told. One man was determined to deceive himself so much he submerged his whole head into the water for three minutes and then called for the hot coals 'for good measure' as he was led away to the ambulance. Or did I just make that up?

No matter. What this study suggests is that for many people self-deception is easy. So if you manage people why not tell them they are very, very good indeed? Because the more they believe, the better they'll be.

Back to the only period in English history when we had three monarchs in less than a fortnight.

Whilst John Dudley was busy believing in his own omnipotence and making the necessary arrangements for Jane's arrival at the Tower, he asked a few soldiers if they would pop up to Mary's house in Hertfordshire and make sure she wasn't going to make a fuss.

He had totally underestimated not only the will of the 37-year-old daughter of Henry VIII but also the number of supporters she had. Mary had escaped and gone east.

She was, after all, the rightful heir to the throne according to Henry VIII's will.

Meanwhile, on July 10th 1553 Lady Jane Grey was brought from Richmond and crowned in the Tower. She and her husband, Guildford Dudley, arrived by barge, and as he was much taller than Jane, she wore stilts under her dress so that when they walked in procession she'd look a little taller.

No, I am not making that up.

Stilts.

On her coronation.

Amazing.

One poor chap by the name of Gilbert Potter criticised the crowd for their lack of defiance at Jane's accession to the throne; he was promptly seized and his ears severed 'at the root' for his lack of compliance.

That must have hurt.

At this point, as the news spread, people were uncertain who to support. Most played a waiting game. On July 12th Mary moved from Kenninghall and set off for Framlington in Suffolk. On the 13th she arrived in Framlington, the ancient seat of the Howards and the strongest castle in the county. Meanwhile, Dudley and his men had arrived in Cambridge only to find she'd fled to Sawston Hall. And when they got there it was only to find she'd moved on again.

So they burned the place down.

Mary was one step ahead in more ways than one.

Dudley had also dispatched six ships containing nearly 1,000 men to Yarmouth in an attempt to arrest Mary but few of them had any naval experience.

There was a bit of a storm so the largest ship, 'the *Greyhound*, lay at anchor off East Anglia whilst the ship's master received enticements from both sides to arrest or support Mary.

If they could find her.

In the end, Dudley tried to play hardball and, desperate for wages, food, water and strong leadership, the mariners broke open the war chest and distributed the money amongst themselves. The ships' crews defected to Mary.

News got through to Dudley.

Anyone who has played sport knows that there is a moment in every game that real competitors absolutely dread. It's the moment when they feel they're about to lose. There's a certain mental tipping point which comes to all people in competition, but the real winners react to it differently.

And it's the same when pitching for business too. Just like a boxing match, there's a feeling that happens at some time in the bout when the competitor feels that he is about to lose; a feeling that today is not going to be his or her day – a feeling that whatever they're doing right now just isn't enough. It's effectively the crux of almost every fight when the adrenalin is still pumping but the strength seems to be draining out of the boxer.

It's arguably the time when sensible people quit. It could also be argued it's when the quitters quit and the losers lose. Surrender seems like a good bet. Few boxers who find themselves with that feeling manage to turn what seems to be certain defeat into victory. I've seen it so often in football matches where a team is 2–0 down at half-time but most of the losing players still believe they can not only get something out of the game but actually win it.

But as the time goes quickly away, so much quicker than the time for the winner, you can actually see the mental belief drain out of the players' faces. As the final whistle approaches, only the real winners still believe they can get something out of it. It is arguably chasing a lost cause but for me it is the sign of a real competitor and sometimes it can be turned around.

And, ironically, the time when the losers are beginning to feel there is no hope is also the time when the winners become complacent and think the match is won. And sporting history is absolutely full of such events. And so it is in life and business. The successful people still believe they can win when the moment comes; when the realisation that they are *about to lose* comes.

But on this occasion Dudley has played for high stakes and he's lost.

Mary and her followers rode into London and imprisoned Jane and her supporters. Mary was the next queen of England.

Jane had been queen for nine days.

Hell hath no fury like a woman scorned. Once Mary became queen in July 1553 Jane and her husband were thrown in the Tower of London. John Dudley was executed for treason at Tower Hill on August 22nd 1553.

Power corrupts.

Absolute power corrupts absolutely.

There is something rather ridiculous really about the monarch. He or she is shut off from the rest of the world, cosseted, fêted and lauded. Yet the business of a king or queen requires them to know their country and its people. And it is the pride of kings and queens that has created so many wars.

To the incongruous farce that is monarchy we have then added hereditary succession. Or, rather, *they* did. No one by birth should have a right to set up his own family in perpetual preference to all others for ever.

But in 1553 you were strung up on a strong length of rope for saying things like that.

Dudley and all the other people around Edward VI were far more concerned with their own personal futures. It was very important to them but the actions taken were not in the best interests of the country or the throne. The actions were in the best interests solely of Dudley and his court. And, as I see it, so it is in most people's lives.

So who was this young man? Edward VI became king in January 1547 and died in July 1553 at the age of 15, never more than a puppet king who was beaten by his tutors and had to beg his uncle for pocket money whilst the Protestant adults were profiting economically from the dissolution of the monasteries. Edward's body lay unburied until August 8th, when it was interred in Westminster Abbey under Protestant rites by his eventual successor, his sister Mary. The Protestant service was carried out by his godfather, Thomas Cranmer, whilst Mary had Masses said for the soul of her young brother at the Tower.

Even in death they were sticking to their fervently held religious beliefs that, in time, would lead to many more untimely deaths.

CHAPTER 10

'Make Mine a Bloody Mary'

Poor young Edward VI never really got a chance to do very much at all. His reign had lasted just six years and he never saw his sixteenth birthday. Fact is, none of us are here very long and most of us achieve very little that lasts longer than our own lifetime.

On the death of Edward in 1553, the eldest daughter of King Henry VIII, the Catholic Mary Tudor, became queen.

Time for everyone to change horses.

Mary was incandescent with rage, ready to change anything and everything her little brother had put in place – and no time to sleep on it.

Despite being given new information as she came to the throne she was in a hurry to change things based on what she believed. People were about to die.

Mary's resentment of her younger brother was obvious for all to see when the first parliament of Mary's reign met in

October 1553. It basically dismantled the whole legal framework of the English Reformation. In addition to completely taking apart the religious enactments of Edward's short reign it also passed an Act invalidating Henry VIII's divorce from Katherine of Aragon thus, in one fell swoop, making Elizabeth a religious outcast and a bastard to boot.

Mary had suffered and it was time to get her own back.

And the small matter of her successor was immediately brought to the fore. She was, after all, 37 years old, single, a woman and had no children. Mary ignored all the advice around her not to marry a Spaniard but, being half Spanish herself, she saw her nephew as the ideal partner to bring England back into the fold of her mother's church. Relations between Mary and Elizabeth very quickly became strained and, despite Elizabeth's affirmation that she was devoted to the Catholic faith, Mary's hostility was deeply ingrained. On November 16th 1553 there was a deputation from the House of Commons formally requesting the queen to marry an Englishman but she seemed set to start her reign simply doing as she pleased.

And as so many chief executives find, it's not easy to break up well-established factions. Not for the first time in history we reflect that absolute power corrupts and that it could all have been sorted out with a sit down, a cup of tea and asking some decent questions establishing each other's motives.

If you've ever been the new kid on the block, you'll know how difficult it is to have your views accepted by the 'established group'. For instance, imagine you've joined a new company and you're attending a think tank to discuss a problem which is new to them, but old hat to you. Something you experienced and dealt with in your previous job. In theory, your views should be welcomed with open arms. But in practice, it's more likely to be open mouths. Who does this upstart think he is? He's only been here five minutes.

This group behaviour is what psychologist Matthew Hornsey from the University of Queensland calls 'unreasoning hostility'. It consists of having your views largely ignored or overlooked.

In my house it's called parenting.

Anyway, to test the theory, Hornsey's researchers asked 200 health professionals for their opinions on criticism levelled at their hospital by an independent observer. However, whilst one half were led to believe that the critic was a newcomer who had worked there only three weeks, the other half were told that they were the views of someone who had worked at the hospital for 18 years. Naturally, the criticisms were identical, with the only difference being the apparent source.

As suspected, the views of the newcomer were thought to carry less weight than those of the old-timer. What's more, their criticism was also seen as less constructive whilst their suggestions were more readily dismissed by the health professionals.

So, as a newcomer, how do you worm your way into a group's affections and begin to generate influence? The answer is to tread carefully and gain acceptance first. Once you become part of the group you can begin to make all manner of recommendations, however absurd. Newly appointed cabinet ministers are prime examples. For instance, you wouldn't ask the Minister for Transport for expert advice on a schools matter. You'd wait until the cabinet reshuffle next week and ask her when she's Minister for Education.

Bottom line is you have to be part of the group. A fully paid-up member of the club.

One of them.

Consciously or otherwise, people want others to value their group as much as they do. So distancing yourself from an old group or employer increases your perceived allegiance to the new one. And criticism from a committed group member is seen as much more valid. In effect, it sweetens the bitter pill of reality.

Of course, the temptation when joining a new group is to try to make a big splash and impress others with your critical perceptions and new ideas. It's what Queen Mary did; thinking that on the grounds she was queen she could do as she pleased and ride roughshod over established groups and their ways of thinking.

But this research tells us that toeing the line in the first instance is often the best long-term strategy.

Even if you are a queen.

Remember, groups are hostile to criticism from newcomers and are likely to resist, dismiss or ignore it. Until you can prove your loyalty.

So if you're a newcomer and want to gain influence and promote change in your new surroundings make sure you get well established first. Because sometimes being right just isn't enough.

The danger for someone who is emotionally attached to the need to be right is that all other perspectives, ideas and suggestions must be 'wrong'. The need to be right convinces him or her of the correctness of their approach but creates suffering for those caught in its wake – most often, partners and family members, including children.

The need to be right can go horribly wrong.

So ask yourself whether you want to be right or happy?

She may have been queen but she was still effectively a newcomer to the group of people who had been running the country.

And before the end of October 1553 she had agreed to marry.

As a child Mary had been betrothed to various suitors. In 1518, when she was two, she was betrothed to the heir to King Francis I, a little later to her cousin, Charles V, the

Holy Roman Emperor and, when Queen Claude of France died, King Francis I offered himself as a husband. On her accession English hopes were pinned on the 25-year-old great-grandson of Edward IV, Edward Courtney. His mother was a friend and confidant of Mary's and the match had the approval of the Privy Council. But Mary quickly made it clear she wanted a Spaniard.

No time to think it through. No time to work out the ramifications.

She married Philip of Spain on July 25th 1554. He was to become king of Spain in 1556.

And yet another newcomer to the group.

From Philip's point of view he'd married his Portuguese cousin as a teenager so why not marry his English aunty? He was 27, Mary was 38. If he didn't marry her then his father would probably get in first.

Familiar?

On marrying King Philip of Spain, Mary was rather grandiosely titled queen of England, France, Naples, Jerusalem and Ireland.

And Mary was to be the second of Philip's four wives; in chronological order they were a Portuguese princess, an English queen, a French princess and finally the daughter of the Holy Roman Emperor. He introduced the Spanish inquisition to the New World. He made it into his seventies too.

Quite impressive really.

So as queen, Mary proceeded to undo many of Edward's Protestant reforms. Mary, remember, was the daughter of Katherine of Aragon and a devout Catholic. She earned the sobriquet 'Bloody Mary' due to the number of Protestant Tudors who were executed during her reign. In 1554 papal authority was re-established in England and the following year Parliament repealed the antipapal laws of Henry VIII and restored the ecclesiastical courts. They didn't restore the church property funnily enough. So lot's of religious persecutions and hundreds burned at the stake, including some big names.

In 1563 John Foxe wrote of Mary's tyranny in his book *Acts and Monuments* better known as *Foxe's Book of Martyrs*.

At the time it was the second most-read book after the Bible. It details the persecutions of people who chose simply to be Catholic rather than Protestant. And that meant that many Protestants came to either fear or hate Catholics. It teaches the lesson we have already learned – that unrestrained power – in this case in the hands of clergy – corrupts both the state and the church.

Those who could read for themselves learned the full details of all the atrocities performed on the Protestant reformers; the illiterate could see the crude illustrations of the various instruments of torture – the rack, the gridiron, the boiling oil – and then the holy ones breathing out their souls amid the flames.

Philip the Spaniard got England involved in the existing war between Spain and France and we lost that little bit of northern France.

Yes, eventually Calais became French.

There was some interesting literary output during Mary's rule. Just before Mary's death another John, John Knox, wrote *The First Blast of the Trumpet Against the Monstrous Regiment of Women.*

Great title but slightly dodgy train of thought. As we've discussed before, once people have a view and an opinion and a belief, they can find evidence to support it. And he weighed in against women rulers, quoting from the ancient fathers and citing various biblical texts to prove that they were incapable of wielding power. To quote from one bit of his book it was 'repugnant to nature, contumely to God, contrarious to his revealed will and approved ordinance' to allow women to have any kind of domination over a nation.

Looking back he must have had an unhappy life, as a woman was to be on the throne for a good 45 years after he wrote the book. What is it that possesses people to have such strong views based simply on opinion? What is it that allows someone to spend a lifetime being unhappy because things have changed and they don't like the change?

We live in a world of constant change. It has always been thus. John Knox was not willing to accept a change that was staring him in the face. A woman is your monarch – get over it. It's a lesson we all need to learn:

If you're not part of the steamroller, you're just part of the road.

A key task if you want to be a leader is to get people to commit to doing things for you; not by getting them to do what you want them to do, but by getting them to want to do what you want them to do. Arguably people ask three questions of their leaders and people back in the 1550s were asking those three questions of Mary.

- Can I trust you?

- Do you know where we are going?

- Do you care about me?

She failed on all three counts. It was her younger sister who was to show the way.

People didn't trust Mary because she made bad, selfish decisions. People thought she didn't care about their right to choose how to worship and she appeared to not really know where she was going. She appeared to have no real vision for a better England.

If you had to sum up Mary's rule in one word it would probably be 'strife'. Mary had her younger sister, Elizabeth, imprisoned at Woodstock Palace. She saw little of her husband, who was 11 years her junior, and she died in 1558 at the age of 42. Childless, alienated, lonely, despised by her husband and hated by her own people.

Mary didn't seem to have a plan other than to produce an heir and get the country back to Catholicism. She wanted to turn back the clock and have things as they were. Well, apart from the fact that she and her cohorts quite liked owning more church land and the monarch being Head of the Church. Not easy giving away what you once had. But she appeared not to have a dream of things getting better; for her or her subjects. She probably laughed at those who did. So here's the corollary:

Never laugh at anyone's dreams. People who don't have dreams, don't have much.

But if you really want to be happy you have to turn your dream into a specific goal, then turn that goal into an action plan and then take action. It always starts with a single step...

Mary's short reign is only now remembered for the murders for which she was responsible; for the bitterness which seems to have been concentrated into her last years.

Mary died almost piously, as she had always lived. In January 1558 she thought she was six months pregnant. At the end of March she wrote her will making it clear that in the event of her death the crown would be left to 'the heirs, issue and fruit of my body'.

By May most people were doing the maths.

By August she admitted that it was possible she wasn't pregnant. In early November she accepted she was actually much nearer to death than childbirth, consented to an agreement that her sister was her rightful heir and asked that Elizabeth keep the Catholic faith.

The word 'forlorn' was quite possibly invented at that time.

In the 12 years from the start of 1547 to the end of 1558 England has had five monarchs, several wars, burnings at various stakes and quite a number of beheadings. Having had a dramatic shift from Catholicism to the Protestant faith under Henry VIII and his young son, we've now had an equally violent move back to Catholicism whilst the monarch rather cynically hangs on to 'the divine right of kings'.

In the 17th century King James's son – Charles I – would go on to famously take his father's struggle with Parliament to unprecedented levels. With his fierce belief in the divine right of kings, the last years of Charles's reign were to be marked by the outbreak of the English Civil War, which would see Britain torn apart as the king's Cavalier supporters took on Oliver Cromwell and his parliamentarian army. The monarchy would be overthrown and a commonwealth established. The second surviving son of King Charles I, James would be the last Roman Catholic monarch and it would be his religious disposition that would lead to his Protestant son-in-law William of Orange to, in turn, depose him.

How things could have turned out differently if Henry had not created 'the divine right of kings', Mary not been so hell bent on insisting that every one of her subjects had to practise her preferred religion. Perhaps the events of Bloody Sunday in Derry on January 30th 1972 would not have taken place? Those events effectively marked the end of the non-violent campaign for civil rights in Northern Ireland and the start of decades of hurt. Events that were discussed for 38 years before the British Government formally apologised for the 'unjustified and unjustifiable' killing of 14 civil rights marchers by British soldiers. Lord Saville's inquiry and long-awaited report showed soldiers lied about their involvement in the killings and that all of those who died were innocent.

What ifs, maybes and if onlys.

On the morning of November 17th 1558 the 25-year-old daughter of Anne Boleyn, Elizabeth, was strolling the grounds of the estate where she lived in Hatfield. And this is the day she is going to be told she has become the queen of England.

The last of Henry's children is coming to the throne.

And she's Protestant. And she doesn't like the Spanish.

Here we go again.

At least this time there will be 44 years on the throne; a chance for some valuable and much-needed stability.

And we all need that. In business and in life. We all need to know what direction we're going in. The more people in business are focused on deciding which horse to back and how best to manoeuvre politically, the less productive work gets done.

People want stability and purpose. And then they can focus on the job.

So what do we learn not only from the bloody pointlessness of Mary's reign but that of her younger brother too? What was gained by this lack of tolerance by one set of worshippers to another? Were the monarch's subjects the better for the cleansing of Catholics from 1547 to 1553 and then Protestants from 1553 to 1558?

And who needs rhetorical questions any way?

In a debate we often hear the retort, 'Well, each to his own' as a rather lazy way of bringing an uncomfortable discussion to a close. Sometimes a conclusion is just the place where you got tired of thinking. 'Live and let live' is the sort of phrase that brings informal debates on religion to an end. But they are not just escape hatches for those who either want to leave a debate or to try and water it down.

Bad guys need locking up. We can't just stand aside. In the second chapter of this book we commented on how William Wilberforce had emphasised that slavery would not come to an end unless people took action; that all that is necessary for the triumph of evil is that good people do nothing. It isn't always better to pursue peace than justice. Just be careful if you frequently speak your mind. You don't have to go around hating and making others feel your pain.

There are plenty of people telling you how to live your life. You don't have to convert people to your way of thinking if their behaviour is legal, decent and fair to others. If people are living their lives by the Golden Rules, if they are learning lessons when they have not done the right thing, if they are treating others well, if they are not omnipotent and have a devil's advocate, and if they allocate time for things that are important but not urgent, then, as they say in Latin, *Ago quod permissum ago, operor non tolerate iniquitas et illigetimi non carborundum.*

And remember that life's too short not to smell the flowers along the way.

Allow me to explain.

Ago quod permissum ago is Latin for 'live and let live'.

But life isn't quite that simple. We can't just hang around while the bad guys misbehave and we have to accept there are things we cannot change. As Reinhold Niebuhr wrote in his now famous 'Serenity Prayer': God grant me the serenity to accept the things I cannot change; courage to change the things I can; and wisdom to know the difference.

Vivere, reservate sed non vivunt in iniustitiam is Latin for 'live and let live but don't live with injustice'.

And *Nil illegitimi carborundum*?

That's right, 'don't let the bastards grind you down'.

And, yes, I know that's not 'proper' Latin but the British Armed Forces have found it works for them over the years.

Many people won't like what you have to say, how you present yourself, or what you do. Accept that the world is not perfect and people don't always see the world as you do. Accept people can have a different view to you. So here's the next lesson

Just because someone's not on the same path as you, doesn't mean they're lost.

Dickens said it back in the the 19th century when he wrote in *A Tale of Two Cities*, 'A wonderful fact to reflect upon, that every human creature is constituted to be that profound secret and mystery to every other. A solemn consideration, when I enter a great city by night, that every one of those darkly clustered houses encloses its own secret; that every room in every one of them encloses its own secret; that every beating heart in the hundreds of thousands of breasts there, is, in some of its imaginings, a secret to the heart nearest it!'

Don't worry too much when you inevitably compare your life to others. People lie on Facebook and Instagram, and even if they're telling the truth you have no idea what their journey is really all about. Sometimes you're ahead, sometimes you're behind.

Live and let live.

But don't live with injustice.

Queen Mary didn't do any of that. She did a lot of fire-branding and needlecraft but the only thing she ever accepted was gifts. If she had accepted that the two religions could live side by side in harmony and had embraced her sister as her natural successor we would now live in a better place. The whole of the UK would look like the Cotswolds but with more services. As it was, in 1558, with her health rapidly fading, she wrote a cynical codicil to her will. She stated that she 'would be succeeded by her heir and successor by the laws and statutes of this realm'. She was referring, of course, to her half-sister, Elizabeth, but Mary couldn't even bring herself to write her name.

Was there ANY fun in her life? Did she ever stop and smell the flowers along the way? Was she ever appreciative of the little things in life? Was there joy in the family? And who needs rhetori...oh, sorry, I've done that one.

Not everyone is cut out for a life in business that has them striving for the next dollar. People have different needs and desires; people have different comfort zones, and some will live a happy and successful life if they pretty much stay in them.

And there's nothing wrong with that.

But regardless of whether you are in business or follow a vocation where money is not the main measure of 'success', you need to smell the flowers along the way.

And for more than just the joy of doing it. When work's driving you mad, go out and talk to the trees. Trees and fields help you think.

Allow me to explain.

It's often said that a change is as good as a rest. And that's particularly true if you've been sitting at your desk all day working on the same project. Apparently, if you go on for too long without a break your brain simply stops functioning properly. So instead of soldiering on, you need to take a step back.

In fact, better still, take a step outside for a breath of fresh air. Because, according to a study by Berman et al., it really can pay dividends.

The bad news is that if your office is in the middle of a town or city, the benefits of a walk may be somewhat tempered by the distraction of passing traffic. But if you can get to a nice piece of tranquil parkland where you can amble peacefully through the undergrowth, threatened only by the occasional woodland creature foraging for food, then you can really reset your brain box button.

Researchers have concluded that the scenery on your little sojourn is a vital part of recharging your batteries. And if you want to return to your desk refreshed and revitalised then you need the healing powers of nature. Magnificent trees, pretty flowers, possibly a lake or pond, maybe even a babbling brook – all have the desired soothing effect. Obviously, if you witness someone setting fire to a sleeping tramp or drowning in a boating lake, that's a different matter. Call the emergency services immediately and then head straight to the pub for a stiff drink.

Marc Berman at the University of Michigan studied the effect of scenery on cognitive function. In the first of his two studies, people were given a mentally tiring task to perform that involved repeating lots of random numbers back to the experimenter in reverse order. And then they were sent out for a walk – one group around a pleasant arboretum and the other down a busy city street. On their return they each repeated the memory test.

The results showed that those who went for a wander amongst the trees improved their performance by almost 20%. By comparison, those whose walk took them down a busy street achieved no appreciable improvement in their score. On the upside, they did come back with fizzy pop and fast food to keep them going in the afternoon.

Even just looking at a picture of a tranquil scene as opposed to a busy cityscape can induce a calming effect that improves performance – though not as dramatically as actually going for a walk in the woods.

You're probably wondering why this is. Well, our attention is grabbed by whatever is most immediate to our survival. For instance, the danger posed by oncoming traffic when crossing a road will be foremost in our mind. By comparison, natural scenes don't engage our 'involuntary attention' and we can let our minds wander free and relax.

Still can't see the wood for the trees? You need to get out more.

It's 1558, it's coming up to Christmas and we have a new CEO. Time for Chapter 11.

CHAPTER 11

Elizabeth I ~
CEO of England Ltd

On November 17th 1558 Elizabeth became queen of England and Ireland. No one could have predicted that this woman would reign until 1603 when she was 69 years old.

And never marry.

She spoke six languages, could instil as much fear as her father ever could and was ready to fend off other claimants to the throne such as her sister Mary's Spanish husband, Philip, and also Mary, Queen of Scots who was Henry VII's undisputed granddaughter. She had sworn to her older sister, Mary, that she was a staunch Catholic to avoid being beheaded but she was Protestant and proud to be Head of the Church.

Basically she was 25 years old and ready for the challenge.

We will see that she has learned the first five Golden Rules and we will learn two more Golden Rules from this remarkable woman's reign.

When Elizabeth came to the throne it's important to remember that whilst only 25 years old she came to the position of CEO of England having learned more than most 25-year-olds about fear, tragedy, disgrace and performance. Back in March 1554 Elizabeth had been conveyed downriver in pouring rain on Palm Sunday from Whitehall assuming that she was going to meet her end in the Tower. But by all accounts, although disgraced and in danger of her life, she never showed the terror in her eyes. A lifetime in the public eye had instilled in her the instincts of a real performer and she played her part as the victim of a great injustice very well. She even staged her own one-woman sit-down strike, ensuring that one of her gentlemen ushers actually broke down in sobs.

She'd learned expediency; she'd learned to go down on her knees in humble obeisance to Mary to save her life and give herself some sort of comfort. Elizabeth had learned to even unceremoniously reject Mary's invitations to court, knowing that the supposedly friendly overtures were more motivated by weakness than affection.

At 25 she had already learned how to use power.

By 1558 she had learned the strategy of acquiescence; she had learned to go with the flow and learned the importance of understanding the motives of her enemies. Like many chief executives, at the start of her reign there was someone else who thought they should have had the job.

And that was the Francophile Mary, Queen of Scots.

Elizabeth's cousin.

But at noon on November 17th 1558 Elizabeth was formally proclaimed queen outside the Palace of Westminster. The English had grown weary of Mary's rule but they knew that the company, England Ltd, had formidable problems and the kingdom was weak and divided. Conflict with the Scottish on one side, the forever ongoing war with the French on the other; overcharged with debt; the people distracted with different and very strong opinions on religion; and no consort for the queen.

Even Calais had gone.

Only three days after her sister's death, Elizabeth is known to have said, 'The burden that has fallen upon me maketh me amazed.' Or, in today's language, 'It's in an even bigger mess than I thought it was.'

Whilst Elizabeth was not the first female ruler of the country, she was the first one who was untroubled by feelings of inadequacy simply on account of her being female. At a time when women were classed as inferior beings, she didn't try to directly challenge the assumptions that women were weak, frail, impatient and foolish but, rather, held that as a sovereign appointed by God the conventions that governed attitudes between the sexes were simply not applicable to her. As we learned from the reign of Henry VIII, everyone needs a good devil's advocate. Every CEO needs at least one colleague he or she can rely on, someone to trust, someone to question their decisions but also someone to stand up for him or her in their absence. And the better the choice the more likely the reign of the CEO is going to be a good one.

Only three days after she came to the throne, and whilst still at Hatfield, she appointed Sir William Cecil her Principal Secretary of State. He was 38 years old and the son of a minor official at Henry VIII's court. He'd been to St John's College, Cambridge, had a grounding in law and had even been briefly imprisoned in the Tower on Protector Somerset's fall.

Cecil had reluctantly endorsed the project to put Lady Jane Grey on the throne but had not been punished by Mary for doing so. He'd remained a clear Protestant yet been able to perform some minor tasks for Queen Mary, travelling to Brussels at her request in order to escort Cardinal Pole to England.

Elizabeth spotted that this man was loyal to her faith but understood about changing horses.

She had learned one of the lessons that Henry VIII would have done well to learn: don't let a little dispute ruin a great friendship.

Cecil had had regular dealings with Elizabeth and, within hours of Mary's death, had already been at work on the new queen's behalf, making arrangements to ensure European princes knew of Mary's death, that the accession went smoothly and jockeying himself into position to be seen by Elizabeth in a good light.

And Elizabeth wanted to show to him that she could be trusted too. They were acquaintances but both recognised the benefits of developing a good, business-based relationship.

Turning an acquaintance into a business associate is hard. Making them a friend is even harder. There are endless reasons why people fail to connect. And just like a marriage can break down, so too can a business relationship. But how do you prevent it from happening? Well, in a personal relationship you could start by sending more flowers and remembering the kids' birthdays. But in business?

Psychologists tell us that we tend to like those people who disclose intimate secrets more than those who don't. Maybe it's a trust thing. After all, if someone's open enough about their penchant for cross-dressing, surely they wouldn't lie about their business plans? However, when someone you've only just met starts pouring out their heart to you, it's a different story. Rather than lend a sympathetic ear, you're more likely to want to change seats on the train or join another supermarket checkout queue. I mean, you only went out for a pint of milk, right?

However, it's also true that people disclose more to those they like. So if that nutter on the train happens to be a major buyer in your industry it's probably best to smile politely and hear him out. Similarly, people tend to prefer those to whom they have made personal disclosures. So again, stick with it.

The trick seems to be not to disclose too much, too soon or too often. Take internet dating. Research suggests that the way internet daters reveal information about themselves provides clues to developing good relationships. Apparently, self-disclosure in terms of earnest conversations about your deepest hopes and fears is to be avoided. So no initial chat about global warming, quantitative easing or social unrest. Stick to your favourite music, food and books and a relationship will be formed more quickly.

Communicating online also gives you more control over the way you present yourself. Webcams, Skype and FaceTime can go so far, but nobody can really see the non-verbal communication that a face-to-face conversation reveals. Like your nervous twitch, constant scratching, or lazy eye. Plenty of time for that over a candlelit dinner. Truth is, it's far easier to construct an online identity with crafted emails and retouched photos. A study by Gibbs, Ellison and Heino concluded that successful online daters tended to use large amounts of positive self-disclosure, along with openness about their intent. The very opposite of many people's actual practice in online dating.

The idea that self-disclosure is important in relationships is no big surprise. But whilst it may be easy to understand in principle, the complexity of the process means it's much harder to do in practice. Generally speaking, it seems best to be open about yourself and honest and clear about your intentions. So don't be afraid to give of yourself if you want to build a good relationship with someone. But remember that the art of self-disclosure is about giving information to others in the right way and at the right time.

In addition to seemingly knowing when to give information to Elizabeth in the right way and at the right time, William Cecil had both an impressive memory and an impressive capacity for hard work. When faced with a complex problem he would actually write down all considerations relating to it – and it was only after he had meticulously examined all the implications of the various solutions that he would venture an opinion. He looked at the danger England faced from invasion by other countries through to the nation's eating habits.

Important but not urgent stuff.

The queen and Cecil forged a unique partnership. When she first appointed him, the queen made it very clear that she wanted to hear his opinions even when they conflicted with her own, and for the next 40 years she rarely took an important decision without consulting him first.

For Elizabeth, Cecil was the ideal partner; the perfect devil's advocate.

He was someone who would stand up to her and give her an alternative opinion but, once Elizabeth had made up her mind, he would then enthusiastically follow her path. And so it was on November 28th 1558 that Elizabeth returned to the Tower in much happier circumstances. For the first public appearance of her reign she was dressed in striking purple velvet. Before the year was out – and despite having one or two Christmas parties – she had dismissed the majority of her late sister's personal attendants and replaced them with those who had been faithful to her. And she remembered she was a Boleyn too. Her Aunty Mary Boleyn's son, Henry Carey, was given a peerage and a nice little manor in Hertfordshire.

Blood runs thicker than water.

She had also developed early on the knack of knowing how much to tell her people about what was going on. During her first year on the throne she kept her Council 'in absolute ignorance' of how her marriage negotiations with the Austrian Archduke Charles were progressing.

And, again, as is so often the case with incoming CEOs, there was a pressing matter that had to be dealt with if the reign was to be a long one. Since mid November 1558 arrangements for her coronation had been set in motion. It was essential for Elizabeth to have a very public and grand coronation to emphasise that the validity of her title as queen of England was beyond question. At this point England was still technically at war with France and, although peace talks were ongoing, there was a concern that the French might put a hold on the talks and argue that Mary, Queen of Scots – who had married the French king's oldest son in April that year – was really the rightful queen of England.

The issue of Elizabeth's legitimacy had hung over her like a heavy cloud since Anne Boleyn had given birth, and French diplomats in Rome had already put pressure on the Pope to declare Elizabeth a bastard. Fortunately the Spanish were also at war with the French and they didn't want to see a girl who was half French on the English throne. And so in January 1559 – only two months after Mary had passed away – the arrangements were rushed through and Elizabeth was crowned. In the two months from accession to coronation Elizabeth had been fairly canny in not giving too much public indication of where her religious loyalties lay. Nowadays politicians do focus groups and rely on Mori polls but in those days Elizabeth was savvy enough to test the ground and, in the event, she was happy to be cast as Protestant and Head of the Church in England. When she was handed an English Bible by a child, she kissed it and plied it to her breast and promised to be a diligent reader of it.

With such gestures going down really well with the spectators, she offered the kind of off-the-cuff witticisms and repartee that Peter Kay and Michael McIntyre would be proud of. Even at this early stage people could see something that was to characterise her reign. She deplored extremists on both sides of the religious divide, which for the extremists meant a lack of conviction in spiritual matters. In fact her faith never wavered; it's just that because she was free of fanaticism she was able to steer a steady course. She only attended chapel once a week and wasn't a big fan of listening to men give her sermons. She didn't see the need to have men of the church act as professional mediators between herself and God.

She's learned the lesson about tolerance and that just because someone doesn't believe in the same religious faith as you, doesn't mean they're lost.

Or wrong.

A lesson that is as relevant today as it's ever been.

Just because someone believes in a certain type of Brexit, it doesn't mean there will be 'a special place in hell' for them, as Donald Tusk, the President of the European Council speculated in 2019.

That wasn't helpful, Don.

Elizabeth could quite rightly see more common ground between Catholicism and the Protestant faith than the differences. And that's what good CEOs do, particularly when bringing together factions within the organisation and the board. She was typically pragmatic in April when the new Bill of Supremacy was given its first reading in the Commons. The original intention that the queen be appointed 'Supreme Head of the Church' had been amended to 'Supreme Governor'. A number of people were unhappy that she should be Head of the Church but Elizabeth was happy to take the less controversial alternative, which still gave her all the jurisdictional powers she wished but allowed the Archbishop of York and others the feeling that they had contributed.

One of the most offensive things you can do to someone is to ignore them. People hate being ignored but Elizabeth was able to stroke some big egos and get everyone on board. For a slip of a girl she seemed to do well on accommodating all viewpoints. When, in April 1559, the Treaty of Cateau-Cambresis had been signed with France, there was peace. And although Elizabeth was unhappy with the loss of Calais, there was some sort of honour in that the treaty the French agreed to sign was that after they had occupied Calais for eight years they would either return it to the English or compensate them financially.

All it really did was give us time to get used to the loss. But within six months she'd calmed down the warring religious factions, had a Council who seemed to be singing off the same hymn sheet and made peace with France.

Plus ça change, plus c'est la même chose.

So imagine that, rather like Elizabeth I, you're a CEO charged with turning around a company. If you believe in *plus ça change*, your enthusiasm for the task in hand may be dented somewhat. But don't despair. Because these days, more than at any other time in our history, the only real constant in both life and business is change. Confused?

Let me explain.

For me, the key to success is not how well you change things but how well you adapt to the change. Businesses now rely more on building good customer relationships than they do on manufacturing. That's because everybody's got access to pretty much the same technology so the only real differentiator is service.

Which brings me to a recent stay at the Four Seasons hotel in Istanbul. I'd just arrived in my room and it was almost midnight.

The telephone rang.

I wrongly assumed it was my wife checking I'd arrived safely in Turkey. Happily I didn't answer it with my customary, 'Hello darling' since it turned out to be the hotel receptionist. She wanted to know if I was happy with the room.

For a second I was tempted to re-enact the scene from *Fawlty Towers* where the guest demands a view of the Hanging Gardens of Babylon. However, I figured her knowledge of the 70s sitcom would probably have only instigated a prolonged silence rather than a belly laugh. Besides the room was perfect and it was very nice to be asked at the start of my stay rather than the end, when they could do nothing about it.

This, I surmised, was a progressive, premium business that took pride in caring for its clientele. And it got me thinking about the service in other hotels and the parallels to be drawn in business generally. As a professional speaker I spend a good percentage of nights in hotels each year. The poorer hotels never ask me what I think of their service. They don't ask if I'm satisfied with the room or if the heating system with a mind of its own caused me to have night sweats again.

Of course, you'd expect things to be different at the Four Seasons since it's a very expensive hotel. After they'd swiped my Gold Card I could actually feel it melting at the edges. And, sure, it would be easy to trot out the old adage 'You get what you pay for' as some kind of excuse. But that, for me, would be missing the point.

They want to improve. They want me to feel valued. They want me to return.

And it's the same for business leaders. Instead of trying to change what people are used to and feel comfortable with, you should concentrate on creating a business environment that makes people feel valued and encourages them to flourish and innovate. Leadership is not just about knowledge and intellect but also about wisdom and creativity. Give people room to grow and experiment and more can be achieved because they feel they are making a difference and are appreciated.

For me the key thing in running a business is to look after your own staff and make them feel valued. Then they'll look after the clients and customers.

So change is going to happen, and with it there can be uncertainty or chaos. So can you influence everything that happens? Well, those who go around saying, 'There's nothing I can do,' or 'What's the use of trying?' are effectively disempowering themselves by implying that nothing can be done to change or influence a situation, and so *never* run the risk of influencing everything. And potential great leaders don't do that.

Churchill didn't promise to fight them on the beaches provided it wasn't too soggy. He might have thought it, but he didn't say it.

Listen to the language you use when conversing with others. Is it positive and encouraging or does it sound sinister and threatening? The style you adopt provides critical clues to your awareness of others and their needs. Good leaders, like Elizabeth I, are aware of other people's feelings and use them to their advantage. In fact, leaders who are often thought to have 'great insight' sometimes have little more than a good understanding of other people's motivations, aspirations, needs and preferences.

When businesses rely more on customer service, perceptiveness is more important than analysis. And when perceptiveness is combined with trust we have a great leader.

And in Elizabeth that's what the country has now got.

Her cousin Mary Stuart was still waiting in the wings and ready for a fight but Elizabeth has made a good start.

CHAPTER 12

Measuring Ladders, Spinning Plates and Being Careful What You Wish For

The end of Elizabeth's honeymoon period as the new monarch was over and it was time for war. In July 1559 Henry II of France had died as a result of injuries in a court tournament and Mary Stuart's 15-year-old husband, despite not yet shaving, had succeeded him as Francis II. Understandably he was somewhat dominated by his 16-year-old Scottish wife and, as she and her family were fanatical Catholics, he saw himself as Catholic too. Mary Stuart rather fancied the triple crown of queen of France, Scotland *and England*. Elizabeth gave clandestine financial assistance to her Protestant nobles in Scotland but it was known that the French were preparing to send reinforcements to Mary, and it was in October 1559 that Elizabeth realised she'd got a fight on her hands.

Elizabeth had three problems. England didn't have the armour; England didn't have the men experienced in war;

and England didn't have the money for yet another scrap with the French. If she failed in her attempt to eject the French from Scotland it was likely that the French, still gloating about gaining Calais, would set sail over the Channel and deprive her of her throne. But if she *didn't* fight the Scots then her cousin Mary may well have gained confidence and come south. The ideal world for Elizabeth was that the French would withdraw their troops from Scotland and Mary Stuart would renounce all claims to Elizabeth's throne. And with the help of her devil's advocate and a bit of luck that's exactly what she achieved.

In February 1560 Elizabeth signed the Treaty of Berwick whereby she promised the Scots that she would 'send men of war there with all speed' if the French invaded Scotland.

By the end of March 1560 the French had duly arrived in Scotland and 8,000 furious Englishmen under the command of Lord Grey walked up towards Scotland. In May they made an attempt to take Leith by storm. But the French won this little skirmish with the English not fully equipped and having scaling ladders that were too short.

Not for the first time Elizabeth had a decision to make.

Stick or twist? Run for home or send reinforcements? There can be no sitting on the fence.

Despite losing 1,500 men, to cut her losses and have them come home with their tails between their legs could well mean the end of her reign. It was not last time that Elizabeth was to show her tenacious nature and the strong sense of purpose that all CEOs need. Fresh troops were sent to Scotland and the siege of Leith continued. She correctly calculated that the resilience of the French on foreign soil would eventually waiver, and that's exactly what happened.

She also got them to measure the scaling ladders properly this time.

As in business it's all the little things that make a difference. Excellence comes from TNTs – Tiny Noticeable Things. Having a good time almost always means somebody has done a lot of work in preparation. The best impromptu events are well planned and someone has taken the trouble to look after all the details.

It's so easy to set off to Scotland with plenty of ladders to scale the walls without checking whether the ladders are the right height. Someone needs to ask these questions when people are planning.

That someone is the devil's advocate.

And at the same time the English had a stroke of luck. In June, Mary Stuart's mother – Mary of Guise – died and the French lost most of their will to resist. Mary was the Queen Consort of Scotland as the second spouse of King James V of Scotland. Not only was she was the mother of Mary, Queen of Scots, at the time of her death she was also serving as Regent of Scotland in her daughter's name. Cecil did a grand job negotiating with the French and in early July the Treaty of Edinburgh was formally signed.

Ironically, the day after peace had been established Cecil received a letter from Elizabeth saying that she now wanted compensation in the way of Calais. She'd got her tail up and wanted to rub the French's noses in it. Looking back, it's probably good fortune that her letter hadn't arrived in time to stop the peace treaty being signed. Cecil was to show great diplomatic skill in also dealing with the not-insignificant issue of the rumours surrounding Elizabeth and the man she loved to be with: Robert Dudley.

Because Elizabeth had also, within the first six months, found someone to make her smile. Attractive, intelligent, cultured and with a good, athletic build, her Master of the Horse, Lord Robert Dudley, was also married, ambitious and flirtatious. He made her laugh.

And we all need someone to make us laugh.

In September 1560 Dudley's wife Amy was found at the foot of a staircase at Cumnor Hall, the Oxfordshire manor house she'd been staying at.

She was dead.

The one thing that was certain was that she'd died of a broken neck – but did she fall or was she pushed? Either way, eventually Dudley was cleared of blame but that didn't stop the rumourmongers. Indeed, the rumour mill went into full operation as to whether or not Elizabeth might actually want to marry Dudley. Elizabeth was intelligent enough to know that he was highly unpopular and that a marriage with one of her courtiers would give rise to jealously, resentment and infighting. Indeed, it could well plunge the country into civil war.

Dudley, remember, had been implicated in his father's plot to get Lady Jane Grey on the throne. However, Cecil could read the signs that, although Elizabeth was obviously attracted to Dudley, her judgement had not been impaired and she was more in love with the throne than with him.

Cecil understood that everyone needs to save face. Everyone needs acceptance time to come to terms with a difficult decision that has to be made. Just as people need time to accept being made redundant or, indeed, grieve. People need time to adjust, reflect and feel that they're making a decision themselves. And in that, Cecil did well.

Elisabeth Kübler-Ross did an excellent job of writing about this 'process' of acceptance to change when she first published the grief cycle model in 1969. Cecil would have been proud of her. Kübler-Ross argued that we all go through seven distinct phases when we face trauma; at first we are shocked and effectively immobilised, then we deny what has happened, then we have anger, bargaining, depression and, before we come to acceptance of the change, we have to 'test' for the meaning of it all. Whether it's death and bereavement, divorce, redundancy, enforced relocation, crime and punishment, disability, injury or bankruptcy, it helps us understand and deal with (and counsel) personal reaction to trauma.

One person's despair, such as a job change or phobia, may not be at all threatening to someone else. Elisabeth

Kübler-Ross, Elizabeth I and William Cecil – and all good managers of people – understand that emotional response, and trauma, must be seen in relative and not absolute terms. We need to appreciate that other people's perspectives are different to our own.

Kübler-Ross was a catalyst. She challenged the 'sweep it under the carpet' and 'don't discuss it' view on dealing with death, bereavement and change. The seven stages are neither linear nor equal in their experience and length. People's reactions to emotional trauma are as individual as a fingerprint.

As people go through the depression phase they need to 'search for meaning' before they can accept things. They need to rationalise and come to terms with why this bad thing has happened to them.

And as a good CEO, Elizabeth I seemed to appreciate that. Certainly she was more sensitive than her brother and sister had ever been.

William Cecil could see Elizabeth very clearly resented all criticism of Dudley and she felt duty-bound to defend him. Indeed, as Dudley was being badly treated she felt even stronger that she should verbally defend him. Cecil advised people not to make matters worse by badgering the queen into a decision. Cecil learned how to live with Dudley, and his policy of placing subtle and often untraceable obstructions in Dudley's path to being her husband, rather than oppose marriage openly, worked well.

Lord Robert Dudley was of course compensated for his love and affection, but he spent his life in pursuit of the forbidden fruit. And Elizabeth learned how to handle the whole situation. As she scathingly once famously said to him, 'I will have here but one mistress and no master.' And it was a maxim that Dudley quite simply had to live with.

Her mind was focused on the main job.

And part of that main job was to focus on the economy. Whilst many were focused on the gossip surrounding Dudley and Elizabeth, Cecil had also been looking at the state of coinage in the country. During the time of Elizabeth's father, brother and sister running the country, the English currency had been undermined and, in 1559, coins were actually worth less than their nominal value because they contained too high a percentage of alloy. Foreign buyers had started refusing to accept English coinage so English businessmen had to pay for goods in pure gold. This, in turn, caused a shortage of gold at home and that had a disastrous effect on the rate of exchange.

Plus ça change, plus c'est la même chose.

The queen took a keen interest in these matters and Elizabeth and Cecil eventually issued a proclamation that all base coins in circulation were to be reduced 'as nigh to their value as might be'. This was a huge undertaking at this stage and there were insufficient quantities of silver at the Mint to produce the number of new coins required.

In the event, the crown made a profit of about £45,000 from the transactions, which involved people bringing in old coins and getting new ones in their place. The revaluation helped English merchants and in July 1561 Elizabeth celebrated her remarkable achievement by allowing them to visit her in the Tower of London.

Unfortunately, whilst presiding over this fiscal success, in early December 1560, Francis II suddenly died and that left Mary, Queen of Scots a widow at 18 years old. Mary was in France at the time and rather fancied coming back to Edinburgh to preside over her people. An envoy was dispatched to ask Elizabeth if Mary might be allowed to pass through England on the way to her own kingdom – and Elizabeth probably made her first mistake. Why not be conciliatory? Why not help her on her way to Edinburgh and even meet her in, say, Richmond, for a nice cup of tea and a chat? They were, after all, cousins and it was an opportunity for Elizabeth to establish the ground rules.

Let Mary rule Scotland and if the French ever come sailing down the Firth or the Clyde with swords at the ready then thay would be more than just cousins. But no, Elizabeth refused her that and Mary was able to turn the rebuff to her advantage, for she could now suggest it was she rather than Elizabeth who was the injured party. She let it be known she would travel from France to Scotland by sea and, by letting the English know of all her plans, effectively said, 'Come and get me.'

In the event, Mary sailed to Scotland and on August 19th 1561 she landed at Leith and quickly set about charming the locals. There only appears to be the author and misogynist John Knox who didn't think much of her arrival.

Once installed at Holyrood Palace near Edinburgh she immediately declared she wanted to make peace with England, but she had a small condition attached to it. Her condition was that Elizabeth agree to reinstate her in the line of succession. And that created an impasse. It's time for either war or a meeting.

Either way it's going to get expensive.

If there was to be a meeting then the nobility accompanying both Mary and Elizabeth would have to have new outfits. There would be substantial transport and accommodation costs – and the not insignificant knock-on effect of what people in France would make of it all. People started busying themselves working out how much bread and beer and wine they'd need. Knights started practising their tilting in preparation for the tournaments which would surely ensue if the queen of Scotland were to meet the queen of England.

On July 7th 1562 Elizabeth gave Maitland the formal assurance that Mary would be welcome for a meeting, and four days later he left for Scotland bearing a sealed document that stated the two queens could meet in the north of England, probably somewhere nice like York and sometime in August or September. Unfortunately, the very next day civil war broke out in France and the offer of a meeting was revoked.

Not for the first time the English monarch sensed a bit of disarray in France and thought it was time to declare war again. The Huguenots in France had secretly offered to give Elizabeth Le Havre if she helped them against the

Guises. Not Calais, admittedly, but Le Havre could be kept as security until they did agree to give Calais back to the English. By the end of August Elizabeth had indicated that the deal was on and, by early October, the first English troops had landed in Le Havre. Unfortunately that October Elizabeth became so ill with smallpox she actually lost the ability to speak. However, she was soon up and well and appointed Lord Robert Dudley a member of the Council. Mary Stuart wrote the queen a nice little letter saying how pleased she was she'd got better.

But what this little illness had done was make everyone consider the issue of the inevitability of anarchy and civil war if she was to die without a clear heir. Lord Robert Dudley had shuffled into pole position in Elizabeth's eyes but that would have been disastrously unpopular. And so it was that by the start of 1563 Elizabeth had four plates she was spinning; four issues that were causing great consternation and debate amongst the English people.

They were as follows.

• The war with France

• The financial implications of the war with France

• The Protestant versus Catholic debate

• The matter of her successor; this having the added issue of who might father her children.

Interestingly none of these debates and none of these issues made things better for the people in England. Surely the purpose of a monarch and a ruling party is to improve the lot of its people? Just as we've seen when we have disunity and disharmony amongst people, so too we make no progress when we get distractions.

We looked at distractions in Chapter 4 and how every year people are killed in accidents all over the world because of one thing: distractions.

Several studies have shown that mobile phones are a leading cause of car crashes and mobile phone distracted drivers are four times more likely to be in a car crash.

People don't keep focused on the most important issue. People lose sight of the real goal and get distracted and begin to concern themselves with issues that affect them rather than pursuing the common goal. So here's the lesson from 1562 I make no apology in repeating:

Always know what the common goal is and keep pursuing it.

Keep people focused on the common goal and don't allow them to get distracted.

But by the end of the summer in 1563 at least one of her problems had been solved; we'd lost this particular war with France. If it hadn't been for the fact that so many people had died it would be comical. Basically there was an epidemic of plague in June and, by the end of the month, 60 soldiers a day were dying of the disease. The windmills which ground the corn in the area had all been destroyed by cannon fire so most of the bakers in the town had either died of plague or couldn't produce food. So when Elizabeth sent fresh troops and supplies, the reinforcements themselves promptly fell sick. But even as the English were making their sorry way back to England, Elizabeth was still keen to remind the French that Calais was soon due to be rendered back.

Needless to say there was plenty of laughter in Charles IX's court.

And then, to make things worse the returning soldiers brought plague with them and there were over 20,000 fatalities in London alone. That, in turn, meant a commercial embargo. The cloth trade ground to a virtual standstill and the crown lost revenue in customs duties until the embargo was lifted two years later.

And for what?

A little bit of France.

However, Elizabeth did what all good leaders should do. She accepted her part in the failure. She took responsibility for the unsuccessful adventure against France. She didn't blame Dudley or Cecil but took it on the chin.

She learned a lesson we referred to earlier, one that Michael Jackson would go on to make such a big hit of. She wanted to make the world a better place; she took a look at herself and made that change.

Big mistake, but, as they say in Yorkshire, 'Top Girl'.

And she learned her lesson. It's often said that you need to be careful what you wish for and in endeavouring to manipulate both Mary, Queen of Scots and Lord Dudley, Elizabeth was to get her comeuppance. Using Dudley as a pawn she conferred the title of Earl of Leicester on him and had her emissaries suggest that Mary marry him. She was probably testing Lord Dudley's affections and toying with her cousin, Mary.

Initially Mary played along saying that she would marry Lord Robert Dudley – now Earl of Leicester – if it also meant the succession to the English throne would pass to her. To confuse things even further Cecil and Queen Elizabeth decided to let Elizabeth's cousin, 19-year-old Henry Stuart – also called Lord Darnley – go to Scotland to meet Mary.

They were endeavouring to obfuscate and confuse the whole issue of Mary marrying and having a child.

Unfortunately, the 19-year-old Darnley was tall, athletic, good looking and a grandchild of Henry VIII's sister, Margaret Tudor.

As was Mary.

Not tall and athletic that is; just a grandchild of Henry VIII's sister.

If Darnley and Mary were to form a real relationship it could be a formidable partnership as their respective claims to the throne of England could be merged. Elizabeth wrongly assumed that even when Darnley was north of the border she would still be in control. Unfortunately for Elizabeth, Mary and Darnley fell in love. And when Darnley had been taken ill by measles, Mary became totally smitten. By the time Darnley had recovered she was besotted and had resolved to marry him, with or without Elizabeth's approval. By May 1565 Mary had conferred a Scots peerage on Darnley. On hearing of this, Elizabeth tried summoning Darnley home but to no avail. Elizabeth even put Darnley's mother in the Tower in July for having 'encouraged her son in his undutifulness' but by the end of the month Darnley was king of Scotland and Mary was his bride.

Not what Elizabeth had planned.

It was an expensive lesson for Elizabeth to learn:

Not only do you have to be careful what you wish for, you have to be mindful of the consequences if your wish comes true.

Or, as Oliver Hardy was keen on saying to Stan Laurel, 'That's another fine mess you've got me into.'

In June 1566 Mary, Queen of Scots gave birth to a son, James, and Elizabeth was to accept Mary's invitation to be godmother to the infant. For now, at least, after years of tension, war, misunderstanding and scheming, the relationship between the two cousins – Elizabeth and Mary – seemed to settle down.

Needless to say, it wasn't to last.

CHAPTER 13

Darnley's Demise, Mary's Imprisonment and the Law of Causality

Time for a recap.

Queen Elizabeth of England saw herself as a bit of a matchmaker and tried to hook up her friend, Robert Dudley, with her cousin, Mary Queen of Scots. She had also sent her second cousin, 19-year-old Henry Stuart, aka Lord Darnley, along for moral support. Unfortunately, being at the peak of his sexual prowess, Henry had other ideas and soon wormed his way into Mary's favour, as she liked to call it. Following a whirlwind romance, the two were married in July 1565.

As Henry said on their wedding night, 'So, I'm the king of Scotland, right?' and then added rather cheekily, 'Love the garter, by the way.'

However, before the end of the year, Mary discovered that her new king was pursuing a life of drink and depravity.

Thinking he was a bit of a comedian, he had developed a stand-up routine that bombed desperately at the Edinburgh Fringe and the whole experience seemed to tip him over the edge. He accused a Scottish-Italian chap by the name of Riccio of having an affair with his wife – and murdered him in cold blood. This shocking news was swiftly followed by the revelation that Mary was expecting. In June 1566 she gave birth to James, a happy, healthy boy with suspiciously olive skin that nobody much mentioned. Four months later, Mary was discussing with her advisors the possibility of divorcing Darnley, and just four months after that he was dead.

He'd been murdered: strangled or suffocated after a bomb went off in the house he was staying at. My money's on suffocation since I've never heard of a bomb strangling anyone. Mary was sleeping somewhere else at the time.

Nod, nod, wink, wink.

By the end of May 1567 Queen Mary had married once more, this time to the Earl of Bothwell.

The Earl of Bothwell's other name was James Hepburn. Bit confusing when people have two names.

Suspicions understandably grew that Mary had organised Darnley's death. She refuted this by claiming she couldn't organise a p** up in a brewery and spent the next three months trying to prove it. Maybe she was honest in her protestations; maybe she wasn't. But, just as in business and indeed all relationships, it's not enough to be honest.

You have to have verisimilitude – the appearance of honesty. And if your husband has just died, perhaps appear just a little sad. No wearing bright colours, that sort of thing. Lay off the bingo for a while too. Looking back, she didn't try hard enough to find her first husband's killers. And so people talk and gossip. And here's the next lesson for us all:

It's not enough to be honest; people have to believe that you're honest. You must have verisimilitude.

Many Scots were in uproar. Not only did they feel that Mary hadn't done enough to find Darnley's killers, she was now marrying someone they didn't approve of. History has a habit of repeating itself.

Time for another fight.

Not surprisingly, Mary, Queen of Scots and her new husband had to leave Edinburgh sharpish. However, on June 15th 1567, just as the royal forces were beginning to prepare battle against the dissidents, Mary agreed to surrender. Bothwell literally galloped away, escaping to Denmark where he heard the bacon was especially fine; nice and crispy, just the way he liked it. Unfortunately, on his arrival he was imprisoned by the king and died completely insane 11 years later.

And no, I am not making that up.

Mary was incarcerated at Loch Leven and that left Elizabeth in a quandary.

In many respects, Darnley's death and Mary's demise suited Elizabeth as Scotland was now run by a clique of Protestant lords who were keen to be on good terms with their English neighbours. But at the same time, if the Scottish lords were permitted to bring down their own monarchy then perhaps Elizabeth too could be divested of her regal status?

So, like all good CEOs, she had to make a decision.

Needless to say the French felt duty-bound to get involved. King Charles IX of France tried to ingratiate himself with the Scottish lords and on July 24th 1567 Mary was forced into signing an abdication statement. Her 13-month-old son, Prince James, was crowned king of Scotland. He cried continuously throughout the ceremony and filled his nappy at least twice.

I'm just reporting the facts.

Elizabeth knew that there was a good middle ground between war and apathy. She still withheld official recognition of the new regime in Scotland but had overseen constructive talks between the English and Scots on border security and had written to the king of Denmark asking if Bothwell could be sent back to Scotland so he could stand trial, unaware that he was now insane, wearing pretty floral smocks, and answering only to the name of Brenda. Just as things seemed to be getting back on an even keel, Mary escaped from Loch Leven. The Douglas family was responsible for both security *and* the plot to allow her to escape.

Tidy.

There was a window in Mary's tower looking out over the water. A window of opportunity, you might say. George Douglas's cunning plan was to bring a boat up to the window in the night and take Mary down the wall into it. Early on the Sunday evening he'd signalled to Mary across the loch and was duly ready with his boat. When it was dark, he rowed cautiously across the water, and took his position under Mary's window. Meanwhile William Douglas was having his supper in the great square tower with his father and mother.

The keys were lying upon the table. He quietly slipped them into his trouser pocket and then cautiously stole away. He locked the tower as he came out, went across the court to Mary's room, sneaked her out through the postern window, and descended with her into the boat. One of her maids, Jane Kennedy, was to have accompanied her, but in their excitement they forgot her and she had to leap down after them.

It sounds more like a panto than a prison escape.

They threw the keys of the castle into the lake, as if that would mean the rest of the Douglases would be holed up in Loch Leven Castle forever.

They rowed hard all night and landed safely on the south side of the loch, far from Kinross. Several of the Hamilton lords were waiting for her, put her on the back of a horse and galloped away. By the end of the week Mary found herself at the head of an army of 6,000 men.

Wondering what to do with them.

She rode further south, shaving off her hair to avoid recognition, and intended to throw herself at the mercy of Queen Elizabeth. A fortnight after her escape Mary crossed the Solway Firth and landed at Workington in Cumbria.

So now Elizabeth was faced with a dilemma.

If she refused to help Mary, Mary may well go to France. And if the French were to help her she would feel indebted to them and the French would be in league with the Scots against the English.

Elizabeth could hardly detain Mary in England against her will as she'd consistently said that a monarch should be allowed to reign. And you have to do what you say you are going to do if you want to maintain your reputation.

The Scots were claiming that Mary was guilty of her first husband's murder so they put pressure on Elizabeth to have her deported back to Scotland. However, Elizabeth decided to buy herself some time by arranging for Mary to be holed up in Lord Scrope's castle at Carlisle.

That really was his name.

He was a small chap, difficult to spot with the naked eye. A sort of micro scrope.

Elizabeth let it be known to Mary that she was sorry for her predicament but unable to meet her personally on account of the murder charge which she assumed was without foundation. Elizabeth even sent her a fresh supply of clothes – her cast-offs. Elizabeth had learned one of the Golden Rules; always have a devil's advocate. And it was Cecil yet again who was able to outline in detail the various options that Elizabeth now had. So Elizabeth reverted to one of the basic laws of negotiation: don't give anything away without getting something in return.

Mary was told that if she was cleared of Darnley's murder, Elizabeth would do all that she could to allow her to regain her royal status. However, there were conditions. In return she was to sign an alliance with England precluding her from making a claim on the throne during Elizabeth's lifetime. She was also to give up Catholicism and revert to the *Book of Common Prayer*. Plus, if she could do anything to stop that damn Tattoo every year, that would be a bonus. With Mary having agreed to all points but the latter, there was to be a trial at York with Lord Herries and the Bishop of Ross representing her.

In January 1569 proceedings came to a stalemate. Mary couldn't be found guilty unless she had put forward a defence – which she refused to do. Elizabeth had played the game well. She'd achieved her aim of disgracing Mary without actually passing judgement on her as a queen, and had avoided formally labelling Mary as an adulteress and a murderer. She was moved to Tutbury Castle in Staffordshire where Elizabeth hoped the security arrangements were better than those at Loch Leven.

Needless to say Mary Stuart's incarceration in an English castle heightened the tension between France and England and gave the French a ready-made grievance if they fancied declaring war again. And whilst relations with France were not in a particularly friendly state, things with Spain were about to get a little bit hairy too.

In November 1568 several Spanish ships carrying treasure towards the Netherlands were forced to take refuge in various English harbours as there were a number of ill-meaning pirates in the English Channel at the time. Elizabeth issued a permit for the goods to be carried from Plymouth and Southampton over to Dover where they could then be transported to the Netherlands. But then she discovered that it wasn't actually the property of King Philip at all; he was being lent it by some merchants from Genoa.

Naturally, she did the only decent thing a monarch could do and kept the treasure for herself. Spain was pretty much at war with Holland and Elizabeth didn't think this would hamper the war effort. However, for every action there is an equal and opposite reaction and several English ships were seized. So in a tit-for-tat manoeuvre all Dutch and Spanish ships in English harbours were stopped from sailing in January 1569.

And Mary, Queen of Scots was obviously still putting her oar in too.

Fortunately, not literally. There was no man in a boat but she did have access to pen and plenty of paper. In September

1568 she had written to the wife of King Philip of Spain saying that if they were to help her she would, in turn, ensure that her son James would marry Philip's daughter and that Catholicism would be returned to England. She also enquired if that apartment on Majorca was still available for the last two weeks of August?

Thomas Percy, seventh Earl of Northumberland, secretly visited the Spanish ambassador in January 1569 and suggested that the recently widowed Philip II should take Mary Stuart as his wife. Thomas himself having an axe to grind as he felt the queen's confidant, Cecil, had too much power and had converted to Catholicism himself two years earlier.

As is the way with office politics, Percy's three allies – the Earl of Westmoreland, the Duke of Norfolk and Lord Lumley – plotted against Cecil but were reluctant to actually speak to the CEO herself. The members of the cabal deluded themselves that they were all-powerful and busied themselves with politics rather than getting on with their jobs.

The Queen tackled the problem head on.

Elizabeth wasn't prepared to discard her loyal servant and devil's advocate simply to appease her rivals. She spoke to them directly and explained that Cecil was to stay but did take on board some of their misgivings about certain issues. She also spoke directly to Norfolk when she found out that he was planning to be Mary Stuart's new husband. Word spread and he himself became an outcast at court.

I think there's a lesson for all of us here about office politics – which often comes down to struggles for power and respect coupled with people being willing to snipe behind people's backs but not talk directly to the relevant people. Get out of the office, sit down, have a cup of tea and chat directly.

Anyway, in September 1569 the Duke of Norfolk left London for Kenninghall, his house in Norfolk, and on October 3rd he was stopped en route and put in the Tower by order of the queen. Good CEOs know when to appease and when to be direct. They need to know when to quell a rebellion and when to let things run their natural course and go with the flow.

The law of causality states that for every action there's an equal and opposite reaction and in November 1569 Northumberland, Westmoreland and the Sheriff of Yorkshire, Richard Norton, went in to Durham Cathedral, tore down the communion table, ripped up the English prayer books and set off south. They assumed that they would be next after Norfolk to be put in the Tower. On November 22nd Elizabeth ordered that the Earl of Shrewsbury should move Mary Stuart to Coventry so that she wouldn't be liberated by the northern rebels and proclaimed queen.

That's right; she was sent to Coventry.

Meanwhile the northern rebels had reached Clifford Moor in Yorkshire, not to be confused with the big shopping centre, Clifton Moor, in York.

And then they began to have second thoughts. The Earls of Cumberland and Derby hadn't come on board as they'd anticipated, and when they looked behind them their army consisted of a few ill-disciplined farmers who were terribly excited but didn't have any weapons, just pitch forks. They'd heard Mary had been sent south, they were getting short of money, winter was coming and by the end of November they'd got cold feet.

Literally and metaphorically.

Before Christmas they'd told their ragtag and bobtail assortment of supporters to 'make shift for themselves' and they went back north to Scotland. By the end of 1569 Elizabeth had seen off the rebellion.

A lot had happened in the five years since Elizabeth had sent her friend and confidant Robert Dudley to Scotland with the plan to have him marry her cousin Mary Stuart. Mary had married a different cousin, then married a fruit cake who had probably killed her first husband, had given birth to a son who had become king, had been imprisoned and was now, under Elizabeth's jurisdiction, holed up in a castle in Coventry where nobody would talk to her.

If only the Head of Security at Loch Leven had done his job properly. If only Norfolk hadn't desired power so much that he wanted to marry Mary and become king. If only Henry VIII had stayed with his wife and not met Anne Boleyn. If only Henry VIII hadn't married Anne Boleyn. If only Anne Boleyn had been content with the Catholic religion.

If only Sid Smith hadn't been late for that physics exam.

What ifs and if onlys and maybes...

It's 1570 and at the start of the new decade the only thing that's constant is change. Mary is to remain in prison for another 17 years and destined never to meet the queen of England.

Elizabeth has other fish to fry and a lot of decisions to make.

CHAPTER 14

Decisions, Procrastination and Succession

Decisions, decisions, decisions. Every day, we all have to make them. Sometimes they have to be 'snap', other times we can afford them more consideration. Occasionally they're hard, sometimes they're easy. The trick, quite obviously, is to get them right more times than you get them wrong.

But how?

Sleep on it. That's right, it really does work. You see, the subconscious mind is brilliant at sorting out all the pluses and minuses associated with making a complex decision. That's because, unlike the conscious mind, it has a greater capacity to process lots of different information and doesn't get sidetracked with preconceived ideas or notions. Instead of jumping to a conclusion, it weighs up all the variables and leads you more often than not to the correct solution. That's why so many successful businessmen rely on their instinct or 'gut feel' to tell them what to do.

Of course, there'll always be a place for the rational, conscious mind to make decisions. If there wasn't we wouldn't have to get out of bed in the morning. We'd just have to work out how to get rid of the bedsores. And that's one problem that can't be solved by sleeping on it. For instance, the conscious mind is very good at applying clear, concrete rules. Like figuring out that if we pick up a hot coal it's going to smart a little. But ask it to compute a complex problem with lots of variables and it gets in a bit of a lather. We sweat, we panic, we feel dizzy, we go down the pub, have a few drinks and go home to bed. Then, miraculously, the next day, everything becomes clear and we have the answer.

The only problem now is remembering the question.

And here's the proof. Psychologist Ap Dijksterhuis of the University of Amsterdam conducted a series of experiments to compare conscious and subconscious thinking. People were given 12 bits of information about four big topics and asked to make a decision. Each topic had a clear 'best decision' that the researchers were looking for. The first group had to decide immediately, with no time for analysis; the second were asked to reason the problem through before deciding; whilst the third group were given the information and then immediately distracted with another subject before being asked to make a snap decision.

This third group, who had only ever been given the chance to think about the problems subconsciously, consistently arrived at the best decision. So the next time you arrive home in the wee small hours and stay awake half the night concocting a story to tell your partner, don't be surprised when they jump to the right conclusion the next morning having been furnished with only the barest of details. It's a gut thing.

Fact is, the bigger the decision, the more important it is to sleep on it.

It's a lesson 'Queen Bess' would have benefited from learning.

Because the 1570s were a difficult time for Elizabeth. At any point there seemed to be a good chance of a war against Scotland, the Netherlands, Spain or, of course, France. As early as January 1570 the Earl of Moray was assassinated which left the Protestant party in Scotland without a leader. Mary, Queen of Scots was in prison and there was a huge dilemma as to whether or not she should get involved and run the risk of the French siding with the Scottish. It seemed an unlikely alliance; haute cuisine on the one hand, battered Mars bars on the other. But as the saying goes, stranger things happen in deep fat fryers.

In May 1570, Elizabeth dined with the French ambassador, and over the main course hinted – without really making a promise – that she would start discussions aimed at putting her cousin back on the throne. And then, looking down at her plate, added, 'Crikey, is that all you get?'.

And that perhaps was one of her great attributes. Speaking the truth, I mean. Not dissing French cuisine. Probably more so than any other monarch, Queen Elizabeth told the truth and did what she said she was going to do. And if you're going to live your life by that mantra, then you don't make false promises, empty threats or commitments that are going to be difficult to fulfil.

By July 1572 the breach between England and France was wide enough to consider completely breaking off diplomatic relations. Consideration was even given to passing a law making it illegal to eat a croissant in public. However, shock horror, by the end of the decade she very nearly married a Frenchman. It seems to be the decade for either marrying a Frenchie or going to war with them. Of course, if you really want to inflict suffering and misery, marriage is really the only sensible option.

Or you could do both.

Again, throughout the decade, she stuck to one of the Golden Rules of always having a good devil's advocate. In fact, she now had two. Naturally, Cecil was still there – newly promoted to Lord Burghley of Horse Trials. But now there was also Walsingham, who offered opinions which she didn't necessarily like. 'But that's the idea of a devil's advocate, isn't it?' he would protest, as he was carried kicking and screaming from the room. Secretly though, Elizabeth seemed to admire his incisive mind and was consistently willing to listen to information she didn't want to hear. He just had to shout a bit louder from the anteroom.

Like all good CEOs she would listen and give the impression she was at least taking the other person's concerns seriously.

In addition to the presence of Mary, Queen of Scots, the threat of war from neighbouring countries and the matter of the succession, she also presided over a fairly impressive cost-cutting exercise. By 1572 she really had turned the monarchy's economy around. Elizabeth's net annual income from feudal and ecclesiastical dues, customs duties and crown lands had dropped from over £200,000 a year to less than £135,000 a year. She'd started with a debt inherited from her sister Mary, had to finance various expeditions to Scotland and France but still managed to get the economy back on an even keel.

Full marks.

So by 1572 things were going quite well with France. At least they agreed to stick to their side of the Channel and we agreed to stick to ours. Charles IX had asked Elizabeth to be godmother to his daughter, which was nice, but then upon his death two years later things seemed to go downhill again. Unfortunately, his successor was Henry III who had been king of Poland for the previous few years and, more importantly, was anti-Protestant. Elizabeth had been given the opportunity to marry him but had given him the brush-off. So at the end of that year, Lord North led a small group to France to try and establish whether the new French king's intentions towards England were as hostile as they might have feared.

And that made things worse.

Elizabeth even thought about taking an army to France and the thorny subject of Calais came up again.

Back in September 1572, she'd sent Sir Henry Killigrew up to Scotland to suggest to them that it was quite a good idea to take Mary back, stage a trial, and then execute her for crimes she'd committed when she was on the throne there. But the Scots weren't happy at the idea of doing Elizabeth's dirty work and were far too busy with their own civil war which was really starting to hot up. By 1575 the Spaniards were ready to repossess the Netherlands – all to do with late payments – but the French were keen on having it too since they'd heard about the wacky backy and how everyone there was really chilled and laid-back. Meanwhile, the queen was getting older.

Perhaps the single most pressing issue for most people at court at that time was the matter of succession. On the one hand, there was Mary, Queen of Scots and her son James. On the other, there was Elizabeth whom most people felt still had time to marry and produce an heir. For the thick end of 30 years she'd had various suitors put in front of her, starting with Thomas, Lord Seymour of Sudeley, when she was only 15. And probably the last great attempt for her to marry was towards the end of the decade. None had thus far measured up.

And then she met the Duke of Alencon.

Francis, Duke of Alencon, was the son of Catherine de Medici, Queen Mother of France, and a brother to the French king. Having been born in March 1555 he was 24 to Elizabeth's 45 years of age.

I'm saying nothing.

The negotiations were based on the mutual needs of England and France to make an ally of each other, with a few of Elizabeth's personal needs thrown in for good measure. The traditional European alliance system whereby England was united with Spain was rapidly deteriorating, and England needed the support of France if she was to protect herself against Spain.

The duke had sent his man Jean de Simier to England to present his case. De Simier had the rather grand title of Chief Darling to Monsieur and seemed to do a pretty good job with Elizabeth. It's worthwhile reminding ourselves that Elizabeth's biological clock is ticking and maybe time has actually run out. She's still trying to find a husband and she's still fussy about how negotiations take place. As always, Elizabeth was absolutely insistent that she must see her possible suitor before she could agree to a betrothal.

Perhaps her father had told her about the fiasco with Anne of Cleves?

However, the French, being a canny lot, were reluctant to have Alencon come over and risk the embarrassment of being turned down. Plus, there was the question of expenses. Ferries weren't cheap in those days. Then there was the small matter of Alencon being a Catholic, and one of their conditions was that Alencon would be crowned king of England immediately after the wedding and endowed with a large pension payable for the remainder of his life, regardless of whether he remained king. His descendants were later to run several British banks and had a similar clause written in.

All this made it very tough for Elizabeth to agree to his terms, particularly when all she requested was that he wore carpet slippers in the house and gave up garlic.

The alliance might stop a war with France but we'd never get Calais back. Alencon and Elizabeth eventually met in August 1579. And what the queen found standing in front of her was a disfigured young man under five feet tall. She referred to him as 'my little frog'.

Not a good start.

And so by the end of the decade Elizabeth was 46 years old and still unmarried. Was it procrastination over tough negotiations or was it a good decision? Well, the finances were in better shape; we were not actually at war with anyone; Mary's still banged up in jail; and a little bearded man from Devon called Francis Drake has been plundering, sailing the globe and generally getting up the noses of the Spanish.

Procrastination is probably the most popular criticism of Elizabeth. And you'll not be surprised to know that there has been quite a bit of psychological research done on the impact procrastination and the incompletion of tasks has on us all. It dates back to the 1920s when the Russian psychologist Bluma Zeigarnik gave some children puzzle and arithmetic tasks to do. She then interrupted one-half of them mid-task and allowed the other half to complete the tasks. Shortly after, only about one in ten recalled the completed tasks and slightly less than that remembered the same number of each.

But 80% remembered the interrupted tasks.

And a whole body of research has repeatedly found that individuals of all ages tend to remember uncompleted tasks far better than completed ones. We also tend to remember negative experiences and feelings longer than positive ones. Basically, there seems to be little motivation to recall jobs we've finished, whilst there's a strong investment of interest in unfinished projects. If you collect things you probably know the items you still want, and don't remember as well what you've already found.

We tend to think more about the rooms in our house that need decorating rather than the rooms we have taken several weeks to paint. So given we are more likely to remember what we don't complete, especially the negative, while we tend to not remember what we have completed, the 'Zeigarnik effect' – as it's now known – impacts on our lives every day. The stress you have from everyday hassles and frustrations often stems from incomplete tasks.

Procrastination is not good for you. So finish tasks, take satisfaction from making a productive difference, savour your successful completions and you will have greater inner peace.

Perhaps if Elizabeth had dealt with the matter of succession and what to do with Mary, Queen of Scots, she might have had a happier life.

I'm a fan of Elizabeth. She was an effective CEO. But not only was she guilty of procrastination in dealing with

Mary, Queen of Scots she was also guilty of something psychologists call 'confirmation bias'. Allow me to explain.

In a world of uncertainty, the one thing that most of us find comforting is being right. Or, should I say, believing that we're right. Often this involves ignoring any facts that don't quite fit with our view of things and, instead, concentrating on those that do.

Politicians have always done this whenever they're faced with making a tough or controversial decision. Or faced with 'fake news'. This act of looking for positive evidence to support your view is known as confirmation bias, and it creeps into all sorts of areas of our lives.

Take self image. Everybody loves a compliment. 'Hey, you're looking really well!' works equally well with men and women and would have most people feeling better about themselves and positively about you. But what if someone *did* insult you and called you a loser? Believe it or not, some people welcome insults that confirm their view of themselves that they suck at something.

A study by Professor of Psychology, Bill Swann, found some people actually seek out information confirming their own view that they are lazy or slow-witted or not very good at something.

Over the years, confirmation bias has picked up the blame for all sorts of dodgy beliefs such as the existence of UFOs, the validity of the moon landings and the events surrounding the deaths of JFK and Diana. In fact, way back in the early 19th century, doctors treated any old disease with blood-letting. Because patients sometimes got better, doctors conveniently ignored all those who died and figured it must be doing some good. Fortunately, it's the doctors who have got better these days.

The only way to fight confirmation bias is to think up and test out an alternative hypothesis. But although this sounds easy to do, it's not in our nature. It's no fun thinking about why we might be misguided or misinformed. It takes a bit of effort. We don't like reading anything that challenges our political beliefs or criticises our favourite film or team. And, more importantly these days, some people find it hard to accept how different people choose to live their lives.

So as I say, in business, trying to sell to people who already have a firm, negative view is part of the challenge that confirmation bias sets us. The key is not to tell them they are wrong – typically all that will do is not only firm up their own view but also leave them with a negative view of you.

You have to ask questions to help them challenge their own view. Ask them what evidence there is that supports their view, and keep asking questions. Elizabeth just stuck to Plan A as far as Mary was concerned and looked for support to confirm her view she was best keeping Mary locked up.

Either way, at the start of 1580 the king of Portugal died suddenly with no heir. Bizarrely, his last words were

'I can't breathe, I can't breathe, there's no air...' Philip of Spain took this opportunity to send an army across the Portuguese border and England could do nothing but watch helplessly as he absorbed the rich Portuguese empire into what was already a pretty extensive organisation.

Alencon had taken up the offer of becoming Prince and Lord of the Netherlands and power was shifting yet again.

But before we pick up the story again in 1580 it's worthwhile outlining the careers and achievements of the three best-known names of Elizabeth's era, and how it was she who invented what we now know as the National Lottery.

Time for Chapter 15.

CHAPTER 15

Francis, Walter and William

During Elizabeth's reign, it's fair to say that her subjects included a number of great talents who served her well. However, those destined to leave the most memorable and lasting legacy were William the Writer, Walter the Explorer and Francis the Pirate. And like all good CEOs, she allowed each of them the freedom to do what they did best. So Francis would spend his days plundering the high seas, Walter would explore far and wide and William would churn out one blockbuster after another.

So before we return to the thorny issue of how Elizabeth deals with her cousin Mary and her tiresome plots – she was a keen gardener – here's a brief pen picture of the three main men in Elizabeth's life. Plus a brief introduction to the National Lottery.

Don't worry, all will become clear.

FRANCIS DRAKE

Francis Drake was born in Devon in 1540. He went to sea at an early age and was 18 when Elizabeth came to the throne. He didn't particularly want to but his parents didn't like him hanging around the house. At the age of 27, he made one of the first English slaving voyages as part of a fleet led by his cousin, John Hawkins, bringing African slaves to work in the 'New World'. However, on the return journey, the expedition was attacked by a Spanish squadron who were out looking for target practice. The bad news for Drake was that only two ships survived the attack. The good news was that he was on one of them. And from that day on, Drake became a lifelong enemy of the Spanish.

In the 1570–71 pirate season, Drake made two profitable trading voyages to the West Indies. In return for slaves, he exchanged anything the locals couldn't get enough of. A year later, he commanded two vessels in a marauding expedition against Spanish ports in the Caribbean. They retaliated by beating us in a hastily arranged rematch. In later years, Drake went on to see action in the Pacific Ocean and captured the port of Nombre de Dios on the Isthmus of Panama. He returned to England with a cargo of Spanish treasure, 600 Panama hats, plus a reputation as a brilliant privateer.

In 1577, Drake was commissioned by Elizabeth to set off on an expedition against the Spanish colonies on the American Pacific coast with the specific instruction to bring back no hats, just treasure. He sailed with five ships, but by the time he reached the Pacific Ocean only Drake's flagship, *Pelican*, was left. Slightly shocked when he turned around to see nobody alongside him, he quickly scaled down his plans from major league marauding and pillaging and plumped for a spot of petty pilfering instead. His ship was later renamed *Golden Hind*.

Among his many achievements, Drake became the first Englishman to navigate the Straits of Magellan and he sailed further up the west coast of America than any European. Unable to find a passage, he turned south and then west across the Pacific. His travels took him to the Moluccas, Celebes, Java and then round the Cape of Good Hope. He'd successfully completed a circumnavigation of the globe and ensured that the Spanish and the Portuguese were not having it all their own way.

During the 1570s, he sailed to Panama, led raids on treasure houses and ambushed mule trains in Peru. He robbed towns and vessels along the South American coast and, in particular, the Casa Fuego. He claimed a bit of California for the queen and generally ingratiated himself with her whilst making himself enemy number one with the Spaniards. In September 1580, he sailed triumphantly into Plymouth harbour with a boat full of Spanish goods. Castanets, pot matadors, wicker placemats, stuffed donkeys, etc. With the *Golden Hind* neatly docked on the south coast, he headed up to London to personally present Elizabeth with his *pièce de résistance*: a crown studded with emeralds plus a diamond cross. Slightly suspicious, the queen tested it with her teeth before paying Drake handsomely and declaring, 'Crikey, it's real.' And then added, 'You can keep the castanets.'

Elizabeth knighted him aboard the *Golden Hind*, much to the annoyance of the king of Spain.

In 1585, Drake sailed to the West Indies and the coast of Florida where he ransacked and plundered several Spanish cities. On his return voyage, he picked up the unsuccessful colonists of Roanoke Island off the coast of the Carolinas, which was the first English colony in the New World.

In 1587, with war against the Spanish imminent, Drake entered the port of Cadiz and destroyed 30 of the ships the Spanish were assembling against the British. A year later, he was a vice admiral in the fleet that defeated the Armada. Drake's last expedition, with John Hawkins, was to the West Indies. This time the Spanish were ready for him and the venture ended in disaster when he was struck on the head by a series of well-aimed cricket balls. Drifting in and out of consciousness, suffering from dysentery, and occasionally muttering, 'No ball,' and 'Surely, that's a wide,' Drake passed away on January 28th 1596 off the coast of Puerto Rico. His body was buried at sea.

Quite a guy.

A bad one.

But good for his CEO.

WALTER RALEIGH

Drake's relative, Walter Raleigh, was also born in Devon – 14 years after Drake so he was just a toddler when Elizabeth became queen. He studied law at Oriel College, Oxford, just so that in later life he could be sure of what he was flouting. In 1578 he sailed for America and in 1585 he created the first English colony, now known as North Carolina. It was whilst exploring North America looking for gold that he discovered both potatoes and tobacco. Given that neither looked very attractive hanging from a chain around your neck or fashioned into a brooch, it was a while before their true worth was realised.

Raleigh had first come to the attention of Elizabeth in 1580 when he went to Ireland to help suppress an uprising in Munster. Later, using his newly discovered root vegetable as a substitute for a tennis ball, he invented the chipped potato when it went straight through the strings of his racket. Knighted in 1587 for his services to road transport and the potato snack market, Raleigh became an MP in 1584 and received extensive estates in Ireland.

However, things started to go wrong for Raleigh when he embarked on an affair with Bess Throckmorton, one of the queen's ladies-in-waiting. I say 'embarked', because it was a bit like a cross-channel ferry. Roll on, roll off, and you're there before you know it. Anyway, by the following summer, Bess was well and truly pregnant with Walter's child. Raleigh was caught between a rock and a hard place. He could stay and do the decent thing or high tail it out of town in the dead of night. After much soul searching he announced to Bess that he had a flat and would be staying. She thought he meant a place to live but he was referring to a puncture. They secretly married in the autumn and she gave birth in the March. It was all very hush hush, apart from the birth which was punctuated with a few muffled groans. Although he constantly denied to Elizabeth that he was both married and a father, it was only a matter of time before she discovered the truth.

You may be able to sweep something under the carpet for what seems like an eternity but eventually the skeleton will pop out of the cupboard.

People also need closure before they can move on. They need to know the facts of what happened before they can come to terms with things. That's why we need public inquiries. And if people think the wool is being pulled over their eyes they react.

When, in 2009, MPs' expenses claims were found to have included clearing a moat, maintaining swimming pools, a 'duck island', fitting mock-Tudor beams to the front of a house, buying trouser presses, bath plugs, dog food, lawnmowers and, in one case, a packet of Hobnob biscuits, what galled us, the hoi polloi, was that the MPs had all signed a declaration with every claim that they had incurred these costs (and I quote) 'wholly, exclusively and necessarily' to enable them to perform their duties as a Member of Parliament. But where were the checks that this was the case?

And when, in 2009, the Prime Minister apologised on behalf of all political parties for some of the 'mistakes' made he saw no irony in the fact that no 'mistakes' had been made where MPs could and should have claimed for *more* than they did...

Fact is, if you are always honest you don't have to remember anything. Life becomes a lot easier.

We want to know the truth. We want honesty. Particularly when things have gone wrong. We want to hold people to account.

The beauty of always being honest is that you don't have to recall what you said to someone.

Whereas whenever you lie, you *always* have to remember in case you're asked again. There are the deceitful whoppers often designed to save a bit of money, and the little white lies usually told to save someone's feelings. For example, 'No, of course, your bum doesn't look big in that' is more likely to precede a successful evening than if your answer includes a reference to, say, a baboon or a sumo wrestler.

The truth is, lies are very difficult to detect. Even the classically studied tell-tale signs are no real indicator. Today, people rarely fidget or look away when they're lying. They don't scratch the back of their neck, act nervously, or change the pitch of their voice. If they touch their nose, it's probably itching. If they touch yours, you're standing too close.

So how do you tell? Well, years of researching real police interviews allowed Dutchman Aldert Vrij, Professor of

Applied Social Psychology at the University of Portsmouth, to provide some guidance about what non-verbal signals represent. Firstly, it's important to consider a person's natural behaviour. A friendly, gregarious, outgoing character who turns up on your doorstep asking to borrow an axe is more likely to get assistance than someone who's a dead ringer for Hannibal Lecter. Similarly, introverts or socially nervous people sometimes give the false impression that they're lying. As a teenager I would often fidget nervously when chatting up a girl, even though I was deadly serious about the proposition. Even the bit about the custard.

Vrij's researchers concluded that the way to spot a lie is to study someone's behaviour when telling the truth, and then to compare this with their behaviour when suspected of lying.

Lying places high cognitive demands on an individual, and the more awkward questions asked, the more pressure they feel, and the more physical signs they display. This is basically how a lie detector works, highlighting the difference in things like facial movements, heart rate and sweat glands.

Of course, if you have a meeting with your boss and you need to know her *real* plans for next year, it's probably not the done thing to wire her up first. So here's a tip. Rely on your intuition. If you're a sales person it should be finely honed anyway. If you're in a meeting and something doesn't quite *feel* right, it probably means that something *isn't* quite right. Either that, or your underwear is on back to front.

In a nutshell, implicit or broadly unconscious processes can be more effective at detecting a lie than conscious directed thought. It's a big nutshell, granted. So if you want to be sure of the truth, ask someone to recount the story over and over again. And don't forget to look out for the TNTs – Tiny Noticeable Things – that are different, as well as any discrepancies in the answer. As they say on the telly, the truth is out there.

Moses said it. If you commit a crime, you run the risk that it will haunt you forever, even if you aren't found out. If you ignore the lesson in life that you should treat people as you would like to be treated yourself, it can only lead to misery and regret. The ultimate result of all ambition is to be happy at home. If you aren't happy in your own skin, you aren't happy.

Raleigh couldn't keep up the deceit forever and by May the secret was out and he was under house arrest. He had committed the fundamental sin of making Elizabeth look stupid and, understandably, she took exception. Raleigh failed to appreciate the gravity of what he'd done and assumed he could sweet talk her round. But in August 1592 he and his wife were sent to the Tower. Being a simple girl, Bess thought they were spending a weekend in Blackpool, so incarceration in a small cell came as a bit of a shock. Despite being released before the end of the year, neither was readmitted to court.

Not for the first time, a man who had power had become greedy and complacent, which started the infighting. He'd alienated too many people with his arrogant ways and there was no sympathy for his plight. To use Raleigh's own eloquent words, he was 'like a fish cast on dry land, gasping for breath with lame legs and lamer lungs'. Then he ruined it by adding, 'like maybe a carp or some bream'.

In an attempt to regain favour with the queen, Raleigh set off to discover El Dorado, the fabled 'Golden Land' thought to be somewhere near Venezuela. It ended in disappointment but it got him out of the house for a while.

When Elizabeth died and James VI of Scotland became James I of England, Raleigh was accused of plotting against the king and sentenced to death. This was ultimately reduced to life imprisonment of which he served just 12 years. During his time in the Tower he wrote the first volume of his history of the world. In 1616 he was released to lead another expedition to search for El Dorado but the expedition again ended in failure. The last straw came when Raleigh defied the king's orders to attack Spain and instead spent a fortnight in Benidorm sunning himself. On his return to England the death sentence was reinstated and Raleigh's execution took place in October 1618. Some people gasped as his limp body was taken away, others couldn't help but admire his tan. Even in death he managed to appear healthier than most of the onlookers.

Raleigh lied, he crossed the CEO and paid the price.

WILLIAM SHAKESPEARE

William Shakespeare was born in April 1564 when Elizabeth had been on the throne for six years, and was but a young man when Drake and Raleigh were strutting their stuff. His father, John Shakespeare, was a member of the local government in Stratford. By trade, he was a moneylender and once appeared in court when it was discovered he was charging interest rates in excess of 20%. Not uncommon then. In fact, not uncommon now. At his trial the judge gave a stern warning of the perils of money lending. 'Neither a borrower nor a lender be; for loan oft loses both itself and friend, and borrowing dulls the edge of husbandry.' 'That's genius,' said young William, eagerly scribbling it down. 'I can use that beauty.'

During his own lifetime, William Shakespeare was better known as an actor than a playwright. He didn't go to university and there are great gaps in his whereabouts for chunks of his life. When he was just 18, he married 26-year-old Anne Hathaway. His plays are racist, sexist, regularly include incest, half-truths about former monarchs and have women dressed as men and men dressed as women.

Although Elizabeth was an active and generous patron of the theatre, and Shakespeare's company was selected several times, there was probably little or no relationship between them. His fame and popularity would come a long time after they were both dead.

Shakespeare once wrote that 'All the world's a stage, and all the men and women merely players'. Not bad for someone who never left England. Of course what he was really saying is that life is all about relationships. And that's obviously just as true today.

However, the question is not whether it is nobler to suffer slings and arrows. That's an easy one; avoid them at all cost. The real question is do we act our part simply to achieve our objectives, or are we influenced by how we think others view us?

This idea that other people's expectations about us directly affect how we behave was examined by Dr Mark Snyder from the University of Minnesota. Acknowledging that one of the quickest ways people stereotype each other is by appearance, he set up a series of 'blind dates' whereby couples chatted to one another via headsets but didn't actually meet.

Having read this far, you will now know that most good psychological experiments involve a certain amount of sleight of hand. Two fistfuls in this case. You see, psychologists know that it's human nature to assume that people who are very attractive are also more sociable, humorous and intelligent.

So, men were given a photograph of the woman they were going to chat to. Except, of course, the photograph wasn't genuine. Half were given pictures of real stunners and half of women who were somewhat more challenged in the looks department. So, would the women pick up on the vibe given off by the men and unconsciously fit into the stereotype they had been randomly assigned? That's to say, would the 'beautiful' women actually be more friendly and sociable, and would the 'less attractive women' be dull and uninteresting?

On analysing the audio tapes, independent observers concluded that the 'attractive' women did indeed exhibit more of the behaviours stereotypically associated with attractive people: they talked more animatedly and seemed to be enjoying the chat more. In short, they conformed to the stereotype the men projected on to them. It seems people really do sense how they are viewed by others and change their behaviour to match this expectation.

The world is a stage. *Expect* your fellow players to like you and think well of you. It really could help the relationship.

So how does that help us to get on with people better? Well, understanding that other people's expectations about us directly affects our own behaviour means we have to be very careful when meeting someone new. Particularly if we think they don't like us. Because that negative vibe will influence their behaviour in a negative way.

On the upside, it also means that we can exert influence over the behaviour of others simply by changing our expectations of them. So if we think that they are going to place a big order, then that's exactly what they are most likely to do.

Elizabeth happened to have three great talents in her company when she was CEO of England Ltd.

And I've dedicated a chapter to them for two reasons. Firstly, no 'account' of Elizabeth's reign would be complete without referencing them and the remarkable contribution they made to her reign; and secondly, for the lesson all leaders can take from managing special talents.

Elizabeth showed what all good leaders should do; she let them do what they were good at. She allowed them freedom to express themselves and only stepped in when they were either out of line, not on brief or deceived her.

And there was one other thing that Elizabeth should be given credit for too – our National Lottery. It can be traced back to the 16th century when a jackpot of £5,000 was up for grabs. Back then, of course, there was no mass media to publicise the event and no lottery machines in newsagents. Which is why it took three years to sell all the tickets and announce the winners.

Because there was no Camelot to organise the draw, Queen Elizabeth did it herself. She wrote a letter to Sir John Spencer giving instructions for collecting money, commanding that 'persons of good trust' be entrusted with the prizes. She suggested 400,000 lots be sold, each costing 10 shillings, with prizes to be paid in a combination of gold and merchandise, including tapestries, linens and fine fabrics.

The jackpot of £5,000 is equivalent to £850,000 in today's money and part of the funds raised also went to good causes, just like today. Not surprisingly, since it took so long to organise, the 16th-century lottery pretty soon died out but there were similar ones held between 1750 and 1826. I've actually got a ticket for the latter and the results are due in any decade now.

Fingers crossed.

Time for Chapter 16 and Elizabeth to deal with her troublesome cousin, Mary, Queen of Scots.

Mary's Boy Child, Harlow's Monkeys and the Sixth Golden Rule

Whilst Mary, Queen of Scots had been incarcerated in some luxury in England and Elizabeth was busy spinning plates, Mary's son James, of course, was growing up. Born in June 1566 he was 12 when an ambassador from France went to Queen Elizabeth to speak on behalf of Mary and Elizabeth replied that Mary was 'the worst woman in the world whose head should have been cut off years ago'. She also added for good measure that Mary would never be free as long as she lived. James had had 12 years of being brought up as a Protestant but knowing he had a Catholic mother who had a right to the throne and was being kept at an English prison.

He'd spent his life living with criticism so he'd learned to condemn. He'd been brought up with hostility so he was prepared to fight. As we discussed in Chapter 3, you reap what you sow as far as bringing children up is concerned.

And our next lesson comes from Dorothy Louise Law Nolte who wrote on her eighty-third birthday, 'if a child lives with security he learns to have faith in himself and those about him'.

Fact is, James's somewhat loveless, confusing and strict upbringing had left him marked; as all childhoods leave us marked.

Harry Harlow would have had a field day studying James's childhood.

The famous experiments conducted by psychologist Harry Harlow in the 1950s, where he separated infant monkeys from their mothers a few hours after birth, are still as relevant and as powerful as they were then. He arranged for the young animals to be 'raised' by two kinds of surrogate monkey mother machines, both equipped to dispense milk. One mother was made out of bare wire mesh whilst the other was a wire mother covered with soft terry cloth.

Harlow observed that monkeys who had a choice of mothers spent far more time clinging to the terry cloth surrogates, even when their physical nourishment came from bottles mounted on the bare wire mothers. 'Mother love' is emotional rather than physiological. Harlow showed how love and continuity of care was a far greater determining factor in healthy psychological development than anything else.

When the monkeys in the experiments were frightened by strange, loud objects, such as teddy bears beating drums, monkeys raised by terry cloth surrogates made bodily contact with their mothers, rubbed against them, and eventually calmed down whereas the monkeys raised by wire mesh surrogates did not retreat to their mothers when scared. Instead, they threw themselves on the floor, clutched themselves, rocked back and forth, and screamed in terror.

For the rest of their lives.

In subsequent experiments, Harlow concluded that 'better late than never' was not a slogan applicable to raising monkeys. When Harlow placed his subjects in total isolation for the first eight months of life, denying them contact with other infants or with either type of surrogate mother, they were permanently damaged.

In 1989 when the Romanian dictator Nicolae Ceauşescu was overthrown, the world discovered that 170,000 children were being raised in Romania's impoverished orphanages. Many were adopted by UK families in the early 90s but are still experiencing mental health problems in adulthood. Despite being brought up by caring new families, a long-term study of 165 orphans found emotional and social problems were commonplace.

Some of those who spent less than six months in an institution showed remarkable signs of recovery by the age of five or six, but children who had spent longer periods in orphanages had far higher rates of social, emotional and cognitive problems during their lives.

Common issues included difficulty engaging with other people, forming relationships and problems with concentration and attention levels which continued into adulthood.

This group was also three to four times more likely to experience emotional problems as adults, with more than 40% having contact with mental health services.

So here is the Sixth Golden Rule.

THE SIXTH GOLDEN RULE:

YOUR CHILDHOOD IS NOT YOUR FAULT.

I'm not proud of being brought up in a small mill town in the north of England. But I'm not ashamed of it either. It's just where I'm from. It's just what it is. I had a happy childhood. You may have had a terrible childhood or awful parents and bad experiences, but your past does not have to rule your present. Psychologists, psychiatrists, medical experts and survivors all agree that, given the right knowledge and skills, people have an absolutely astonishing ability to repair mentally and emotionally from past hurts. If you were unfortunate enough to suffer emotional or physical abuse, criticism or neglect, you did not cause it, so don't blame yourself.

I appreciate this is much easier said than done, but knowing that what happened wasn't because you were a bad child, and knowing that you have a tendency to operate out of guilt is a good place to start reprogramming how you think and feel about yourself and how you relate to others.

And Mary's son James?

No father, didn't know his mother but was always expected to behave; he'd learned duplicity at a very young age. And so just short of his fifteenth birthday he started flexing his own muscles. He organised that the Anglophile Earl of Morton – who had acted as Regent during the early part of James's reign – was arrested and charged with the murder of his father. No real evidence but this is 1581 and you don't really need much evidence.

James ruthlessly had Morton executed on June 2nd 1581. He was 14 and had just put down his first marker.

Word spread and not for the first time Elizabeth deferred taking action.

Was Elizabeth guilty of procrastination in dealing with Mary, Queen of Scots or did she make the right decision by waiting and thinking it through? Certainly it must be one of the longest periods of time that any CEO has ever taken to make a big decision. Fact is, there was a quick, easy, ready-made solution to the problem of Mary, Queen of Scots and that was to have her executed when she first entered England.

But like so many other knee-jerk reaction decisions that haven't been thought through, it would have been the wrong decision. It's a lesson for us all. There is a quick, easy, ready-made solution to every problem. Unfortunately it's usually the wrong solution.

People fall into one of two categories when it comes to getting things done. There are those who draw up to-do lists and manage their time efficiently, and there are those who never have enough time. The former tend to get things done whilst the latter are busy procrastinating. Putting off today what they'll probably also put off tomorrow.

This issue of procrastination is such a big one hanging over Elizabeth's legacy – indeed, one that so many people struggle with – it's worth further examination. We all have an item or two of unanswered correspondence in our in-tray. Things we don't really want to deal with like writs and summonses, parking fine demands and county court judgments. (It's never dull in my office, I'll tell you.) Two weeks later and the unanswered correspondence is officially a 'pile'. Two weeks after that and it's become a hillock. Wait further and it's a mountain. You get the idea.

In Chapter 14 we looked at how and why procrastination is bad for your general health and well-being. So how *do* we stop procrastinating and start getting things done? Well, a psychological study by McCrea, Liberman, Trope and Sherman appears to demonstrate that how quickly we act depends upon how we construe the issue. Apparently, there are two kinds of construal: abstract and concrete. Suppose you have a major presentation that you are putting off planning. An 'abstract construal' is one where you imagine the audience laughing along and clapping rapturously at the end. Whereas a 'concrete construal' is where you imagine specific feedback on your performance such as a flattering email from your boss.

So researchers devised a study to get participants into one of these two modes of thinking. Half of them were shown a painting and told it was a good example of neo-impressionism in which the artist was using order and colour to invoke emotion and harmony. This is a good example of an abstract construal. Meanwhile, the other half were just shown the detail of the painting and told that it demonstrated a particular technique of using contrasting points of colour to build up an image. This is a concrete construal.

Both groups were then asked to complete a survey and return it within three weeks. Their answers were irrelevant – the only thing the researchers wanted to discover was how long participants took to return the questionnaire. This was their measure of procrastination. Those thinking about abstract issues such as emotion and harmony took almost twice as long to return the survey as those who were thinking about specific techniques and details. Taking on board findings from other research in this area the answer is clear: to avoid procrastinating on a task, you should keep the ultimate abstract goal in mind but also focus on its details and use self-imposed deadlines.

If you can be bothered.

Elizabeth was very definitely bothered. But she also understood the ramifications of making a 'final' decision as far as Mary's life was concerned.

And there's something else. Back in the 16th century, most things happened very slowly. Nowadays, everyone is in such a rush. Traffic moves faster than ever, apps provide shortcuts to our favourite sites, and we communicate electronically with just about everyone. And we expect a more-or-less instant reply. Through great leaps in technology life has moved on at a blistering pace. But is it any better?

In the 1960s, well before the internet, email and even mobile phones, Paul Simon's famous lyrics urged us to pace ourselves. 'Slow down, you move too fast, you got to make the morning last,' he sang. He went on to suggest, 'Just kicking down the cobblestones, looking for fun and feelin' groovy.'

Who doesn't love kicking cobblestones?

In business, as in life, it's often assumed that fast is best. We want faster broadband, shorter journey times, instant gratification, and everything yesterday. But according to Aesop's fable, slow and steady wins the race. So which is it? The hare or the tortoise?

On Wall Street, traders are greatly rewarded to think and act quickly, earning millions for their clients when they correctly anticipate a market shift. But when some sleep-deprived trader puts a comma in the wrong place at two in the morning and pays $20 a share for Lehman instead of $2...well it all goes a bit pearshaped. More speed, less haste, as another saying goes.

Thing is, the more expert somebody is at a job, the faster they work. They don't rely on slow, system two thinking. Instead, their fast, intuitive, visceral heuristics take over. And like you, I don't really know what that means but it sounds good so I'm going to keep it in. On the other hand, highly conscientious, highly neurotic people are likely to be slower but no less accurate. So, in an industry where precision really matters, the 'tortoise' is probably the more highly prized employee. In fact, in business, you can deliver a solution so quickly that the client thinks you haven't thought it through. The problem is we think the world wants us to be a hare not a tortoise, so we wrongly equate speed with accuracy.

I bought Sarah Millican's autobiography for my book club last year and it was voted our worst book EVER. The last chapter was a recipe for a chocolate cake.

Her granny's.

It was obvious that her publisher had asked for another 5,000 words sharpish. So she turned to her granny's recipe book because that was the fastest way to generate the numbers. But it wasn't the best way.

Ultimately, greatness is about performance, not speed. It's about the thing that's produced, not the velocity with which it's produced. For you, then, not being in such a hurry, finding a slower way to hone your power and realise it in a truly excellent way might make much more sense.

To misquote Simon, 'Spend time with no deeds to do, no promises to keep, I'm dappled and drowsy and ready to sleep. Let the morning time drop all its petals on you. Slow down, you move too fast.'

Back to the 16th century.

James intimated that he would declare war – probably along with France too – if Elizabeth went ahead with the execution, but he didn't actually say that in so many words. What he did do was suggest very clearly that they would only resort to hostilities if Elizabeth excluded him from the succession.

Not for the first time we see that potential monarchs look after themselves even when their mother's life is at stake.

Mary was eventually put on trial in October 1586.

Nineteen years after Elizabeth ordered her arrest.

She was alleged to have conspired to kill Elizabeth. The queen of England had asked her advisors if they could not arrange for the 'natural' death of the queen of Scotland, but as those requests consistently fell on deaf ears she eventually pulled the trigger.

Or, to be more specific, ordered the axe to be wielded.

A leading member of the Catholic gentry, Anthony Babington had become heavily involved in a plot to overthrow Elizabeth. It was his damning correspondence with Mary, detailing the planned events and overseas invasions backed by Mary's written consent, that finally gave Elizabeth's Walsingham his chance. With a few more incriminating references falsely added into copies of the letters for good measure – presumably to ensure the absence of any mitigating loopholes – they had the evidence they needed. As we saw with Anne Boleyn, once a decision is made extra evidence is found...

On February 7th 1587 Mary was informed that she was to be executed the very next day. Mary didn't lose her composure before the execution. She made her will on the dawn of the day of her execution. She was executed in the Great Hall of Fotheringhay Castle at 8 o'clock on February 8th.

She was 44 years old when her head was struck off with two blows of the axe. She was 24 when she'd been first imprisoned by the Protestants in Scotland so she'd been held captive for nearly half her life. James was not yet 21 and although many of his subjects were up for a fight with the English, he could see that he could become the first king of England and Scotland.

And that would come to pass before he would reach his mother's age at her death.

Mary, Queen of Scots had actually been betrothed to Edward VI in 1543 when he was six years old.

It might have turned out so differently.

What ifs, if onlys and maybes.

In the spring of 1587 Mary, Queen of Scots was no longer a thorn in Elizabeth's side. Instead, the French and the Scots were an ever-present threat and the rumours from Spain suggested they were preparing for war. To make matters worse, Elizabeth's army in the Netherlands hadn't been paid for several months and were growing restless. Even the delights of the local nightlife were beginning to wear thin.

King Philip of Spain hadn't been happy with the treatment of the English Catholics and even less impressed when Elizabeth killed his sister-in-law. On top of this, Francis Drake was getting right up his nose with his exploits in what was described as the 'New World'. He also believed that he had a claim to the English throne. His minions trawled through the genealogy and reminded him that Edward III's son, John of Gaunt, had married Constance of Castille. 'And your point is?' he replied impatiently. 'Well, your mum was their daughter which makes you the grandson and rightful heir. And you never shut up about the weather.' Few could argue with their logic.

When people have an opinion they look for evidence to support it – and they can usually find it. That summer Philip signed a treaty with the Pope which stated that after he had conquered England he could crown whoever he wished as king or queen provided that the new ruler converted the country to Catholicism. The pontiff also offered the thick end of a quarter of a million pounds towards Philip's expenses, payable only after Spanish troops had landed in England.

It would have been best if this plan had been kept a secret. However, Pope Sixtus V was an old man and, a little worried he might pop his clogs at any time, he decided to let the cardinals in on the top secret plan. And, naturally, they told everyone else.

Eventually, the queen found out and sent Francis Drake to Spain to have a good look at what they were plotting. She advised him to attack as many Spanish ships as possible and to apply suncream liberally. Not one to drag his feet, Drake was soon in Cadiz harbour causing mayhem. He burned or captured nearly forty ships and was clearly loving his work. Within a short time he had sunk around a hundred Spanish ships and burned all their precious cargo. Still a Guinness World Record.

Sensing that he was on a roll, Drake left his base at Cape St Vincent and sailed for the Azores where he captured the *San Felipe* and brought it back in some triumph to Plymouth. His navy somewhat depleted, King Philip was forced to revise his plans. He decided to sail right up the English Channel and anchor at the picturesque seaside town of Margate.

Who said war can't be fun?

CHAPTER 17

Elizabeth ~ 'A Weak and Feeble Woman'

And so, as 1588 drew nearer, more and more English people were worried what the new year might bring and began hastily changing their holiday plans.

A 15th-century mathematician, Regiomontanus, had read the heavens and concluded that in 1588 there would be either a universal consummation and a final dissolution of the world – or, at best, a general alteration of principalities, kingdoms, monarchies and empires.

Naturally, people started to worry and wish they were better educated. So many long words.

Still, it didn't sound good.

Regiomontanus was the stage name of Johannes Müller von Königsberg. He'd built a portable sundial for Pope Paul II in 1465, gained favour with the pontiff, and his reputation as an astronomer grew and grew even after his death.

In response to Regiomontanus's forecast, the Privy Council ordered Dr John Harvey to write a book saying it was all nonsense and there was no need to panic. He even took the trouble to explain that although there would be two lunar eclipses, the position of Mars within the solar system suggested that there would be no negative issues to trouble them.

People really did believe this stuff in those days.

Some still do.

A psychologist by the name of Leon Festinger came up with the theory of 'cognitive dissonance' in the 1950s. It helped explain why people of strong convictions are so resistant to changing their beliefs even in the face of undeniable contradictory evidence. I myself have some strong convictions but mainly just for motoring offences.

Festinger and his associates at Stanford University heard about a housewife called Marion Keech who had mysteriously been given messages from aliens on the planet 'Clarion' that the world would end in a great flood before midnight on December 20th. Convinced that the aliens would come to their rescue, a group of believers had gone as far as quitting their jobs and leaving their spouses in order to prepare for the evacuation via flying saucer at one minute to midnight. So strong was their conviction that none had sent Christmas cards or bought presents.

Festinger and his colleagues infiltrated the group of nutters – I mean believers – and were probably a little disappointed that, as dawn was on the horizon, there had been no flood, no visits from extra-terrestrials, and no free trip on a flying saucer.

But at 4.45am Mrs Keech had a new vision. Apparently, the world had been spared because of the impressive faith of her little band. "And mighty is the word of God," she told her followers, 'and by his word have you been saved – for from the mouth of death have you been delivered and at no time has there been such a force loosed upon the Earth.' And then she added, 'Have we missed the last Christmas post?'

Fruit cake.

In the late 1960s there was a strongly held belief amongst some that Paul McCartney had died in a car crash and, with the Beatles at the height of their success, the three remaining Beatles simply 'replaced' him with a stunningly convincing and equally talented, left-handed lookalike. People looked for evidence for this theory and could find it. The second line of the number plate on the VW Beetle car behind the zebra crossing on the 1969 *Abbey Road* sleeve read '281F' and was said to mean Paul would have been 28 if he'd lived. He was 27 at the time. A mumbled coda on 1967's 'Strawberry Fields', 1968's 'I'm so tired' and 'Revolution 9', plus McCartney being the only one with his back to the camera on the cover of the *Sgt Pepper's* sleeve and wearing a black carnation in the 1967 *Magical Mystery Tour* ballroom sequence, was all grist to the ridiculous mill. But once people believe something they look for evidence to support the belief they've got.

And can find it.

Ignoring evidence to the contrary.

It's how the brain works and why it's so difficult to convince someone that they are wrong despite all evidence to the contrary.

Throughout modern history there have been many 'conspiracy theories' but all each one comes down to is what evidence you look for. Whether people think JFK was killed by more than one man and whether 9/11, the deaths of Diana, Princess of Wales and David Kelly were all the work of the 'establishment' are down to what they believe and them looking for evidence to support the belief they've got. I don't know the answers to those particular conundrums. I just know there are unanswered questions.

When Theresa May was not allowed to ask Parliament for a third vote on the Brexit deal in March 2019 it was because the then Speaker of the House, John Bercow, had discovered some obscure precedent that the same motion couldn't be heard for a second time without it being substantially different to the first one. He went right back to 1604 to find that. He was looking for evidence to stop it happening and found it. Even though he did need to go back over 400 years.

But before we go back over 400 years again – it might be useful to look at the very positive aspects of belief and how we can benefit from believing in something.

As we know, hotel maids spend most of their day lugging heavy equipment in and out of bedrooms and up and down hallways. In fact, every aspect of their job is physically demanding.

But here's the thing. Most of these women don't consider themselves to be physically fit. In fact, 67% of a group of hotel maids in a recent study by Harvard psychologist Ellen Langer claimed to do no exercise – even though their working day seemed to be one long workout.

So Langer devised an experiment to test if the hotel maids perception of how much exercise they were getting had an effect on their actual weight.

Langer's team measured the maids' body fat, waist-to-hip ratio, blood pressure, weight and body mass index. They found that all of these indicators matched the maids' perceived lack of exercise, rather than their *actual* amount of exercise. And then Langer set about changing perceptions. She divided them into two groups. To one group she explained how many calories were burned off with each task they performed at work. They were also told that this activity met the US Surgeon General's definition of an active lifestyle. The other group was given no information at all. Just told to get on with the job. That's the hotel business for you.

A month later, the researchers returned to take physical measurements of the women and, low and behold, in the group that had been 'educated' about their physical activity, there was a decrease in their systolic blood pressure, weight, and waist-to-hip ratio – and a 10% drop in blood pressure. How come? Well, one possible explanation was that the process of learning about exercise and its effect had somehow changed the maids' routines. However, a post-study survey revealed that none of the maids had changed their routines in any way. So the change in their physical appearance could only have come from the change in the women's mindset.

According to Langer, if you believe that you're exercising, then your body may respond as if it is.

Essentially, it's a placebo effect. Just like when people believe that their medication is making them better when actually all they're taking is a sugar pill. So, in theory, if you believe with great conviction, you might be able to sit around all day eating chocolate and still lose weight.

Great news for anyone who likes the idea of keeping fit but isn't too keen on exercise. Think a hundred or so push-ups and the pounds will drop off. Do it from the comfort of your couch whilst eating a TV dinner and see for yourself.

Okay, so maybe it's not that dramatic, but Langer's study of hotel maids does have some thought-provoking results.

I've already started my own study and it's absolutely delicious.

Back to 1588.

Elizabeth is preparing for war.

Defence preparations were made on land, men were trained, merchant ships were requisitioned and a list was drawn up of likely landing spots by the invading Spanish. By the spring, the Spanish still hadn't shown up and Elizabeth, itching for a fight – though some say it was her cotton sack underwear – was thinking about going on the attack. Wishing to seize the initiative, Francis Drake was first to volunteer. 'I knew you'd be well up for it, Franny.' the queen said.

Well, something like that, anyway.

Perhaps, like all pugilists, she wanted to keep fighting even though it was probably best to retire. However, she was well off retirement age. Plus, she'd spent a lifetime stabilising the country. But despite all her successes, and the fact that England Ltd was in much better shape when she left it than when she arrived, there was still a simmering cauldron of problems left for her successor to ladle.

Although an English fleet set sail for Spain from Plymouth at the end of May, the weather was so bad they were driven back and Elizabeth changed her mind on the attack. 'Do people really come here for their holidays?' she was heard to muse. However, she was worried that the Spanish would sneak up and get England while they were away.

She was probably right.

In July 1588, the Spanish Armada finally left Spain and made for England. A week later it was spotted off the Cornish coast refuelling with pasties. The Spanish had adopted a very complicated defensive formation where the slow and less well armed supply ships were screened by rows of war ships. To the English it must have looked quite daunting, but when you've got Francis Drake on your side you don't fear much.

For several days the English fleet trailed the Armada as they made a little progress around the Isle of Wight. It was Cowes week and the traffic was shocking. The Spanish were weighed down with all the supplies and ammunition necessary for a long campaign and needed to get along-side the English ships. However, the English knew this and wouldn't let it happen, taunting their Spanish foes with renditions of 'Who ate all the pies' long into the night. Eventually Drake calmed them down. 'All right boys, enough's enough.'

At midnight on July 28th, eight English ships were selected and turned into mobile incendiary boats by stuffing them with combustible materials. They were sent towards the Spanish, hoping to dislodge them from their anchorage in Calais. It worked. As dislodgements go, this was pretty spectacular. The Spanish were thrown into confusion. They assumed that the English fire ships were packed with explosives and so cut themselves loose and sailed out to sea. By now the English had the numerical and tactical advantage, plus all the pies.

Fresh ships were called for. In the fog and mayhem of war this order was misheard and 200 bags of chips were delivered. Drake almost blew a gasket and screamed, 'I said ships, not chips!' and then added sheepishly, 'Pass me some sea salt.' With the wind behind them, the English finished up chasing the Spanish Armada all the way to the Firth of Forth.

The Spanish were stuck north of Scotland, low on fuel, low on provisions and low on morale. The tourist board there told locals just to ignore them. You can't please everyone. Meanwhile, James VI had assured Elizabeth he would not befriend the Spanish as he had his eyes on the main prize of the English throne. In August 1558 Queen Elizabeth sailed to Tilbury to review her troops and give her most famous speech.

British history is littered with famous quotes that live long in the memory. From 'A horse, a horse, my kingdom for a horse' right up to 'Football, bloody hell'. The former by Richard III and the latter Sir Alex Ferguson. Although it could easily have been the other way around. But one of the most famous lines must surely be that of Queen Elizabeth I as she addressed her troops towards the end of her reign.

Standing before them in just her nightwear and without a stitch of make-up she declared,'I know I have the body of a feeble woman, but what do you reckon to this new nightie?' Fortunately, she tried out this line on her courtiers earlier that morning and it was generally agreed that it would have far more resonance if changed to, 'I know I have the body of a weak and feeble woman, but I have the heart and stomach of a king, and a king of England too.' Much better.

By all accounts her army cheered long and loud and were only encouraged to stop when she turned her back on them and lifted her attire. This wasn't reported at the time but I like to think it's true. So apart from performing the world's first moonie, what else did she do that day? Well, for me, she tackled head on what's today known as 'the elephant in the room'. Rather than ignore an obvious negative she accepts the unspoken truth that she is just a feeble woman with a bad taste in nightwear. Which means that her enemies will no doubt underestimate her too. But she cleverly counters this admission with a line that all men who have ever encountered a 'feeble-bodied' woman with strong spirits would appreciate. 'But I have the heart and stomach of a king, and a king of England too.'

Feeling herself on a bit of a roll, she decided to motivate her loyal subjects further by pledging that she herself would take up arms if needs be. To demonstrate her prowess she grabbed a crossbow and aimed it at the cheering hordes. This caused them to scatter in a mad panic whilst shouting expletives. Generally though, her actions are thought to have lifted the spirits of her men and challenged them to be as strong as her.

Seventy-three-year-old Reagan used the same technique in 1984 in the presidential debate with candidate Walter Mondale. A reporter asked him if he could function well in the event of a major crisis. Reagan replied that he'd be able to cope and added, 'I want you to know that I will not make age an issue of this campaign. I am not going to exploit for political purposes my opponent's youth and inexperience.'

Touché.

The key lesson? Tackle head on the 'elephant in the room' and turn it to your advantage.

Elizabeth gave people the belief that the tipping point that losers see had not arrived. The English would win. The motivational speech over, and no sign of the Armada returning, she took cheese and crackers with her good friend and cohort, Leicester. His penchant for cheese and habit of blushing uncontrollably in the presence of royalty gave rise to his nickname of Red Leicester.

Still popular today.

By the end of August the camp at Tilbury was dissolved and Elizabeth made dramatic reductions in her armed forces with the carefully chosen words, 'Thanks boys. You're all fired.'

The act of a good CEO but a little tactless, perhaps.

Elizabeth had learned one of the great lessons. Namely, that you need to finish off your opponents when you're in a position to do so. So, following victory over the Armada, she was intent on putting Spain to the sword. In September 1588 she had plans for an expedition under Francis Drake and Sir John Norris but costs escalated.

They finally agreed to ditch the onboard cabaret and make do with deck quoits.

Six months later, the fleet set sail but was back with its tail between its legs within a month. Money had been wasted and estimates of English losses stood at 11,000. Drake and Norris were asked to justify their conduct before the Privy Council and it was some years before Elizabeth entrusted Drake with further military responsibility.

And so the war with Spain was not really finished. Over the next few years the French had their own civil war and Elizabeth actually sent troops to help Henry IV on the understanding that they would side together against Spain. But the men and the money that Elizabeth had poured into her campaign in Normandy had pretty much been squandered and no ground gained. Elizabeth was incensed at the way the French had deceived her, and Henry had not done what he said he was going to do.

In September 1592, the French king presented her with a love token in the shape of an elephant. Elizabeth jumped up and down and clapped her hands excitedly at the thought of what this wondrous gift might be that was shaped like an elephant. And then she realised. 'It *is* a f***ing elephant!'

And then she fainted.

If you were to draw up a list of the very last thing she wanted to concern herself with at that moment, looking after an animal that was very big, very grey and growing at an alarming rate would be at the top of it.

Meanwhile, King Philip of Spain had no time for pachyderms. We don't know that for sure, it's just a hunch.

Instead, he was putting pressure on anybody who might be interested to declare his daughter the queen of France. However, for Frenchmen, the idea of a foreign female on the throne was too much to bear. In the autumn of 1594 Elizabeth sent troops to Brittany which helped rid the Spaniards from their base near Brest.

And all this, of course, was costing England money. Elizabeth's financial position was poor. The cost of the victory over the Armada, the cost of the Portuguese expedition, and financing operations in the Netherlands and France, meant she was spending a prohibitive amount of money. And in 1590 she sold crown lands and also frequently participated in privateering ventures. In 1592 Elizabeth was part of a syndicate that captured the *Madre de Dios*, a great merchant ship loaded with carpets, silk, jewels and spices from the East Indies. Losing men, losing money and a sequence of poor harvests in the 1590s meant that the queen was in trouble. There's also the ongoing matter of unrest in religious terms. And she'd had to have Sir Walter Raleigh arrested too for marrying Bess Throckmorton. Although she did approve of his plans for a Spud-U-Like franchise throughout Europe.

In December 1595, preparations began for another major offensive against Spain. This one was to be a joint Anglo–Dutch affair with 18 of the queen's warships being matched by 18 from the Dutch navy. With additional ships from private individuals, the fleet eventually numbered 150 sails. Times had changed since the days when Drake had first preyed on outposts of the Spanish empire. Back then they weren't so well defended. Now ports were much more strongly fortified. With Drake having died early in 1596 the queen announced the command of the new expedition was to be entrusted to Robert Devereux, the Earl of Essex, and Charles Howard – better known as Lord Howard of Effingham.

You can make your own joke up there.

By April, all the preparations were complete but things changed when news arrived that a troop of Spanish boats were unexpectedly laying siege to Calais. Henry IV of France was unable to defend it and it was clear that unless Elizabeth did something to help, Calais would fall. She agreed, on condition that we could keep it.

What is it about Calais? There's got to be more than just cheap beer and fags.

However, Elizabeth acted too slowly. By the end of the month, Calais had been taken by the Spanish and her dreams of repossessing it had gone. The Spaniards were literally perched on our doorstep whilst the people on the south coast scratched their heads in bemusement.

In June 1597 an expedition eventually left Plymouth led by the Earl of Essex with Sir Walter Raleigh as his right-hand man. The fleet was in Cadiz before the end of the month. Two of Philip's largest warships were destroyed and others captured. The 'Islands Voyage' was an English campaign against the Portuguese colonies in the Azores and was a key part of the Anglo–Spanish War.

However, the voyage was doomed to failure when Essex, defying the orders of Elizabeth, pursued the ships carrying the treasure without first defeating the Spanish battle fleet. It turned out to be the last major expedition sent to sea by Elizabeth and contributed to Essex's decline in her favour. It was also to be her last real attempt to win a decisive victory over Spain.

The crown's resources were overstretched and the queen had no new ways of raising additional money. Although she had her failings as a leader, in particular cancelling possible expeditions and changing the men in charge, in the final analysis it must be said she never withdrew her support from a naval venture to which she had earlier committed herself.

The only serious consequence of her actions was when Calais fell to the Spaniards in 1596. In truth, her main problem was people embezzling the loot she had paid them to seize, and her commanders being reluctant to carry out her instructions to the letter.

Men. We just never listen.

CHAPTER 18

Past Pensionable Age, 'Success' and the Seventh Golden Rule

By the end of the 16th century Queen Elizabeth was 67.

The warmongering with Spain, Portugal, Ireland, France and Holland had consistently swallowed up resources. She'd pretty much been at war for all of her time on the throne and there'd been costs attached to that. During the last years of her reign she attempted to cut down on court expenditure and that created a negative atmosphere both at court and in the country.

There were also various rival claimants to the throne and although Elizabeth never formally endorsed it, it seemed to be James VI of Scotland who would succeed her.

Her father, Henry VIII, had made it clear in his will that should all his children die without having children themselves, then the crown should pass to his sister Mary's children.

But they were the Greys.

Elizabeth had always hated the Grey family. When the eldest great-granddaughter of Henry VII, Lady Jane Grey, was forced onto the throne in 1553 Elizabeth had been officially branded a bastard and banned from the succession. And that's not the sort of thing you forgive and forget easily.

You reap what you sow.

The middle daughter, Lady Catherine Grey, secretly married Edward Seymour, a nephew of Henry VIII's third wife, Jane Seymour, and when Queen Elizabeth discovered the marriage she imprisoned both Catherine and Edward for two years. During Catherine's time in the Tower she gave birth to her first son but Elizabeth refused to recognise any of Catherine's children as legitimate.

And the youngest daughter, Mary, was not to learn from Catherine's and, indeed, her grandmother's mistakes in marrying without the permission of the monarch. She made an ill-advised marriage in June 1565 and her chosen bridegroom could not have been a worse choice, as she married the royal gatekeeper, Thomas Keyes. He was twice her age and called 'the largest man in the kingdom'. A particularly bad match if the reports of Mary's appearance are true and that she was 'very small, crooked and deformed'.

Mary and her husband were both imprisoned although Mary was released in 1572, following her husband's death some months earlier. By then Mary was not only small, crooked and deformed but also old and disgraced. She died in 1578.

Elizabeth's brother and sister had both tried to challenge their father's will and failed. So Elizabeth had the will locked up in an iron casket and threw away the key.

No photocopiers in those days.

In February 1603 Elizabeth gave an audience to the Venetian ambassador and was in good health. But she died the following month of blood poisoning. She was nearly 70 years old.

And she seems to have learned a big lesson in life – that ageing happens. Our bodies age. It's what happens. It's an unavoidable truth. You just do the best with what you've got. Beyond that, do your best to let it go. Enjoying life is really the only antidote to getting older.

But although Elizabeth accepted she was past pensionable age, she had never made a will.

But by this stage everyone knew who would succeed her.

To make a will and name names would, in her mind, create factions and the successor would probably gather forces and rise against the her.

Before the end of March 1603, James VI of Scotland had been proclaimed King James I of England.

When Elizabeth had ascended the throne it was weak, poor, demoralised and suffering great internal strife. Under her tutelage the nation regained its self-confidence, sense of direction and sense of purpose. Despite the ups and downs the reign was fundamentally stable and united, and the company 'England Ltd' was left in a better state than when she took over.

Her country hadn't been invaded and she had died a natural death. Not something that could be said for a lot of monarchs in those days. She'd shown tolerance to Catholics and was regarded as a popular and strong monarch.

As is always the case with good CEOs and good managers, she'd been given a long enough period of time to see her plans come to fruition. She was consistently well advised and she used her devil's advocates well. She did what she said she was going to do and that enhanced her reputation.

She had learned the Golden Rules.

When she died, King James of Scotland came to Westminster to be crowned king of a united Britain. And although the Kingdom of Great Britain would not be formalised until the Act of Union in 1707 under Queen Anne, the two would never declare war on each other as they had done for centuries.

Like Henry VII all those years before, he had brought together warring factions – in this case Scotland and England – by uniting the crown. When James VI of

Scotland became king of England he was 36 years old and had already been married for 12 years to Anne of Denmark, the second daughter of King Frederick II of Denmark and Norway.

When he was crowned king of England he had a two-year-old son who would go on to become Charles I and marry the daughter of King Henry IV of France.

Within two years of James becoming king, Guy Fawkes and his pals would be responsible for a group of English Catholics attempting to assassinate the new Protestant king and replace him with a Catholic head of state.

Plus ça change, plus c'est la même chose.

In the period from the middle of the 14th century to the start of the 17th century, this book has seen much warring with France, despite many English princes having a penchant for young French girls and much blood shed between Catholics and Protestants, and despite many of the protagonists being related. There have been disagreements, broken pacts and promises, much like we have seen since the Brexit referendum over 400 years later.

And we leave the story just as Guy Fawkes' Day is about to become part of our annual calendar and as the New World is beginning to be developed.

Elizabeth, of course, had already left her mark on the New World, with Virginia being named after her.

And we also leave the story with, for the first time, the king of England, Scotland and Ireland being the same person. But despite all these changes, James's son Charles would go on to marry a French princess just as Edward I, Edward II and Richard II had done in the 14th century.

Within a few years of the end of Elizabeth's reign the English set sail for America and many men were lost in the hopeless attempt to keep control of what would become the USA.

Within 100 years the crown itself would be usurped. Did they learn the lessons that we have outlined in this book? An emphatic 'no' to that one. Have we, in the 21st century, learned what we could and should have from this remarkable period in history?

Make your own mind up.

Elizabeth seemed to understand the importance of not losing the lesson when she lost. She had learned what *not* to do from her siblings. She had also shown a tolerance not exhibited by her sister, brother, father and ancestors. She had been tough on dissidents but even with her biggest rival, Mary, Queen of Scots, she had spent years treating her not as Mary would have wanted to be treated – Mary would have had freedom and the crown – but arguably as she would have liked Mary to treat her if the roles had been reversed.

Well, at least she let her live.

In Cecil she had found the perfect devil's advocate. She had listened to his counsel before taking the big decisions. And she ruled the better for it.

She had understood the importance of taking her time over decisions that would cost lives and have long-term repercussions for the country.

Unlike her father.

She allocated time for things that were important but not urgent. Such as what to do with Mary, Queen of Scots.

With the burning (literally in her sister's day) issue of religion she had encouraged people to live and let live. Only the fanatics and bigots hated her for that. She had sought justice and didn't let her detractors at court get her down.

And she lived her life by the seventh Golden Rule.

THE SEVENTH GOLDEN RULE:

DO WHAT YOU SAY YOU ARE GOING TO DO

When you said you were going to do it.

How you said you were going to do it.

And with whom you said you were going to do it.

Always.

I hear people say that the essence of great customer service is to 'under-promise and over-deliver'. I understand the sentiment but I have a problem with it. It's not easy to *over*-deliver every day. Day in and day out.

Just promise.

And then deliver.

Just do what you say you're going to do. If you sign a contract, abide by your commitments.

That's what Elizabeth did.

If you make a promise that you will be at a certain place at a certain time then be there. If you are not there it's almost always because you didn't set off early enough. And that, in turn, usually means you didn't think it was important enough to be there. You had other, more important things to do.

Or, of course, you just don't care.

Or are just plain lazy.

Looking back on running a business I would say that the root of the vast majority of problems with clients, staff and suppliers was that somebody hadn't done what they said they were going to do or someone had misunderstood what, when and how someone was going to do something.

Basically, expectations had not been met.

The reputation you have is the experience people have of you MINUS what they expected of you. It's that simple.

If you say you're going to deliver a product or a service to a customer by a certain date and you don't deliver it, the customer draws the conclusion you either forgot, you are lazy or you had more important things to do.

What other conclusion could they draw?

Do what you say you're going to do.

How hard is this?

Apparently very hard.

I've been in pursuit of excellence for more years that I can remember. My view is that if I can find perfection in customer service and experience, I can define it and share it with audiences around the world.

And in 2019 I found it.

The Tokoriki Island Resort in Fiji is the best I've ever experienced, so over a beer I asked the owner, Andrew Turnbull – a successful Australian businessman in his own right before buying Tokoriki – what were the 'secrets'?

He said there are really only three things to be success-ful: common sense, hard work and people skills. I don't doubt he's right that these are key ingredients to running a successful business but I think he was being overly modest. Personally I think it's a drive from the people at the top and the constant pursuit of excellence. Over a coffee a few days later I asked the Sales and Marketing Director at Tokoriki Island Resort, Patrice Belle, what *she* thought were the secrets to the resort being TripAdvisor's Top Rated Resort in Fiji for four consecutive years?

I told her that my wife and I had observed that each and *every* member of the staff at Tokoriki had learned our names. They had taken the trouble to cross-reference our name against our room number and commit it to memory. So every time we bought a drink, ordered a meal, or checked in for snorkelling or a massage they always greeted us with a smile and first name. I asked Patrice why they went to such trouble and she said, 'Because this is our standard.'

They have set themselves very, very high standards in all aspects and are proud to live up to it. They had just built an area for guests who have checked out but are waiting for the transport back to the airport. A few comments had been made by guests that there was nowhere to freshen up once they'd checked out on their day of departure. So they simply decided to build an area for that very purpose.

They had had a bit of an issue with seaweed being washed up on the beach so Andrew commissioned the *Hoover Suva* and the boat now takes seaweed from the sea.

Every day.

And the staff are the happiest I've ever known.

Anywhere.

They enjoy their pursuit of excellence.

In conversation with Patrice I believe these are the five secrets to excellence and customers having an excellent experience which, in turn, means they return and recommend.

- Excellence is a standard.

- Everything matters.

- Look after all the TNTs (Tiny Noticeable Things).

- Look after your staff and your staff look after your guests.

- Nothing is ever quite good enough so constantly look to upgrade, improve and raise the standards.

So is this approach beyond the reach of other businesses? Could you set such a high standard in your business, maximise your assets, charge a premium and make more money? Is it really possible to satisfy your customers to such a degree that they will always keep coming back for more?

The answer is clear and simple having experienced Tokoriki.

Don't settle for mediocrity, aim for excellence.

Everyone wants to be treated as an individual. Everyone wants to be treated in a special way.

So why don't institutions honour their moral obligations? Why don't politicians live up to their promises?

We crave consistency. We want reliability. We don't want tiresome excuses. We enjoy more relationships with people who care; people who do what they say they are going to do.

'Success' is, of course, different things to different people. It has many meanings depending on what each person is seeking in his or her life, relationships and career.

It would be easy to conclude that, for an athlete, success is winning that gold medal but it would be to miss the point. For many athletes success is getting to 'the next stage' and achieving their full potential. Each individual has to determine the true meaning of success in his or her own life.

But whatever your definition is, the one overriding factor that affects people's opinions of you – and therefore the reputation you have – is whether you are reliable; whether you do what you say you are going to do. Of course there are many examples of people in the arts who are successful and reliably unreliable. But people don't trust them. They know they can't rely on them.

Are they successful in what really matters in life – the relationships we have with the people who are closest to us?

If we aren't trusted by the people we love we are surely not successful. And it's difficult to keep loving someone who is unreliable and doesn't do what they say they are going to do.

The things that really count in your life can't be counted.

It's a lesson many people take too long to learn.

When I ask people all over the world what is the most important thing to them in their life I almost always get 'family' as the answer; particularly those who have their own children. And if your own children don't see you as reliable – if you don't do what you say you are going to do – you are unsuccessful in the most important thing in your life.

One measure of success is how close one comes to accomplishing one's predetermined, self-set goals. Nothing in life occurs just by chance. You have the power to control your life, to control your success and your failure.

We get setbacks of course. But people are there to help us when we do; the closest people to us. But if we are unreliable those people are less likely to want to help. If you haven't shown you care by doing what you say you are going to do, why should they?

You reap what you sow.

Success is about working at something, progressing and having a 'purpose'. It is doing exactly what you want to do with your life providing it's worthwhile, you are happy within yourself and happy with the thought of the future.

Viktor Frankl learned this when he observed the way that both he and his fellow prisoners in Auschwitz prison coped – or didn't – with the experience. As a psychiatrist he saw through a qualified lens how men who comforted others and who gave away their last piece of bread actually survived the longest. His conclusion was that each prisoner became what he was because of an inner decision and not just the terrible camp influences.

Those who allowed their inner hold on their moral and spiritual selves to subside eventually fell victim to the camp's degenerating influence – while those who made a victory of those experiences turned them into an inner triumph. Frankl came to believe man's deepest desire is to search for meaning and purpose.

Expectation, belief and desire are the three powerful forces that come together to help us be 'successful'. If you really want something to happen you have to desire for it to happen first, and you have to not only believe deeply that it will happen, but you have to actually expect that it *will* happen.

Your subconscious mind works on the information and messages you send to it. So not only is it critical that you do what you say you are going to do – because it enhances your reputation and makes you happier (because people don't criticise you for being unreliable) – it also means you are more likely to achieve your goals and aims in life because you have told your subconscious brain that you do what you say you are going to do. And if that means you are going to win the metaphorical gold medal, it's more likely you will be on the podium.

It's natural.

Elizabeth I is one of our best known and most respected monarchs. She took over the running of the country after her father, brother and sister had, in turn, caused strife and deep divisions not only amongst their own people but amongst families. She used Cecil – and others – as a devil's advocate and listened to their sage advice. She made sure she spent time doing things that were important but not urgent and was tolerant of other people's religious beliefs. She endeavoured to never be complacent. She had a 'live and let live' attitude but didn't tolerate fools, nor those people who ignored her or threatened her realm. And she lived her life by the seventh Golden Rule.

Starting with Edward III we have seen 14 monarchs in this book. We have seen the throne switch from white rose to red and back again. We have seen the Plantagenets give way to the Tudors and we leave it as we enter the House of Stuart. The longest reign is that of a woman.

And the most successful.

What of the final lessons to be learned?

Should Richard have been happy with his lot and let the boy king rule? And did he miss out big style in the luxury ice-cream market? Should Arthur have booked a fortnight in Benidorm rather than a weekend in Wales and avoided catching his death? If so, he would surely have been crowned king and Henry VIII would never have ascended to the throne. Should Henry have stuck with his first wife?

Should Guy have kept his powder dry?

Should Walter have just stayed on the farm in Devon?

When Sir Walter Raleigh brought back tobacco during Elizabeth's reign, few at the time could have forecast just how many people would die prematurely. Not only from the impact of tobacco smoke on the lungs and body but also from the fires started by errant cigarettes. Even in the 20th century, few seemed to have any qualms about the potential health risks posed by smoking, first pointed out in a 1929 scientific paper by Fritz Lickint, of Dresden, Germany.

Elizabeth's successor, King James I, described the tobacco habit as 'a custom loathsome to the eye, hateful to the nose, harmful to the brain and dangerous to the lungs'. A scientific consensus on the dangers of smoking did not emerge until the mid-1950s, however.

Almost 200 stars, including two-thirds of the Top 50 box office actors during the late 1930s and 1940s, took the Big Tobacco Shilling, praising brands for their taste, smoothness and ability to provide relaxation. John Wayne, who died of lung cancer eventually, told the public that cigarettes helped his voice.

All for the money.

American Tobacco handed out huge amounts of money to Hollywood stars as part of a massive strategy that ran for nearly a quarter of a century – the intention being to make smoking a symbol of virility for young men and a symbol of femininity and freedom for young women.

And they knew it harmed people.

Andy Fastow knew that his elaborate hiding of the Enron figures would lead to ordinary people losing their pensions. Although when Fastow pleaded guilty and agreed a maximum 10-year prison sentence, he did so in order to reduce his sentence and name others. In the same year Enron ex-chairman Kenneth Lay was still pleading 'not guilty' to 11 criminal charges including bank fraud, share trading fraud and making false statements.

He died before sentence was passed.

Despite the fact that. J Bruce Ismay's coat of arms carried the motto 'Be Mindful' he allowed *Titanic* to sail with too few lifeboats, the workmen in Belfast to install cheap rivets and wireless operators to be more concerned with making money from sending passengers' telegrams than conveying messages about icebergs.

And a coal fire in the three-storey-high coal bunker on the ship.

But he did have a marvellous staircase at the heart of the ship that only sailed for four days.

Perhaps if Bruce had taken his wife of 24 years on the trip instead of just his secretary and valet it might have been different. Perhaps if Captain Schettino hadn't flirted with Domnica Cemortan on the *Costa Concordia* that story might have ended with no deaths.

As we've said before, keep focused on the common goal and don't allow people to get distracted.

It's called work for a reason.

When Catholic lands and properties were seized in the Tudor period the landed, Protestant gentry kept the money and possessions when the country converted back to Catholicism. When young Edward VI was Boy King, Dudley became Grand Master of the Household and Earl Marshal of England but showed his appreciation to the young boy by stealing church land.

Henry VIII's right-hand man, Cardinal Wolsey, embezzled to fund his colleges at Oxford University and only handed his ill-gotten gains back when his number was well and truly up.

Anne Boleyn's father stood aside as his own son was wrongly accused of having sexual relations with his youngest daughter.

Having stood aside as Henry VIII had had carnal relations with his wife and both his daughters.

All so that he could progress his political career and personal power base.

Plus ça change, plus c'est la même chose.

The thread that runs through history is that human greed, hubris and disunity brings about fall.

It was our second Golden Rule.

And although I have usually limited myself to using one company, battle or downfall as an example, the sinking of *Titanic* was such a spectacularly avoidable mess that it warranted more than one appearance in this book.

I guess the final lesson is that life is always going to be a series of choices. And the price you have to pay for making a choice is wondering what would have happened if you had made a different decision. Some good, some bad.

Your place in the world, your meaningfulness, is something you must create for yourself.

Too many people live for no reason and don't see what their purpose is in life. Some see it as making more and more money, others to make themselves famous, or to become powerful; sometimes all three. And whether or not they attain these objectives, they find their lives empty and meaningless. If you don't decide what is worth doing, someone else will decide for you.

What you are doing right now is the thing that you most want to do. You may be thinking that you would rather be on a beach but I would challenge you. If you really wanted to be on a beach, you'd be there. The reason you are not is because you have chosen other priorities in your life; probably good choices like your family, your job and your education.

Even bad consequences are mainly a matter of choice.

So here are the seven Golden Rules for a happy and successful life. Live your life with these rules as your constant companion and you will be more liked by more people, enhance your reputation, be happy, be more successful in what you choose to do and leave this planet the better for you having been here. And that is the purpose of life; to develop loving relationships and make a meaningful, positive contribution.

- When you lose, don't lose the lesson.

- Beware hubris.

- You reap what you sow.

- Always have a devil's advocate.

- Allocate time for things that are important but not urgent.

- Your childhood is not your fault.

- Do what you say you are going to do.

* * *

I never did get to be a civil engineer nor gaze expertly through a theodolite.

And it was many, many years later that I returned to Bath.

I was asked to speak at a conference in that fine Somerset town exactly 40 years after the incident with Sid Smith outside the physics exam. I was drawn to walk around the town and wonder what might have been if I had studied there.

What ifs, if onlys and maybes.

Out of interest, Susan Garlick and I did have a brief relationship.

She dumped me.

Rather like when, on August 16th, 1962, Pete Best was told to leave the Beatles by Brian Epstein.

They had already found another drummer.

Many years later he famously said that he was very happy with his wife and two daughters. That he was happier than he would have been if he had stayed with the Beatles.

Maybe, Pete. Maybe not.

Unlike Pete Best I *know* that it turned out best for me. And I hope it turns out best for you.

I *have* wondered what would have happened if Sid had not spoken to Susan Garlick on that particular day in 1971. I've also wondered what would have happened if the future

King Arthur and his new bride, Katherine of Aragon, had not gone to Ludlow Castle in 1502 and caught a chill.

But that is how it is. And we are where we are. And your childhood was what it was. So we need to accept all that and face the future whilst learning from the past.

We only get a certain number of trips round the sun.

The real secrets to happiness are in acceptance of the things we cannot change and that it's all in the journey, not the destination.

And as for history?

Well it's a bit like life really; it's just one bloody thing after another.

The Rules for a Happy Life

1. When you lose, don't lose the lesson.

2. Beware hubris.

3. You reap what you sow.

4. Always have a devil's advocate.

5. Allocate time for things that are important but not urgent.

6. Your childhood is not your fault.

7. Do what you say you are going to do.

The 50 Lessons

1. Never deprive someone of hope; it might be all they have.

2. You don't know what you've got 'til it's gone.

3. Be in the right state and not in a right state.

4. If you create enemies you create plots against you.

5. Plan for the unexpected and you won't be caught napping.

6. All it needs for evil to triumph is that a few good people do nothing.

7. Your memory is reliably unreliable.

8. If you plant corn, you don't get potatoes.

9. Expect great things and you're much more likely to get great things.

10. Treat others as you wish to be treated.

11. Treat everyone you employ as a volunteer.

12. If you keep your kids busy doing worthwhile things they won't have time to get up to mischief.

13. You don't always need hard evidence that something can be done before you plan to do it.

14. Never write down the words 'I love you'. You can always deny you said it. You cannot retract what you write.

15. If the lawyers get involved, check the small print.

16. If you run a business or manage a team, keep people focused on the common goal and don't allow them to get distracted.

17. All things pass.

18. People who are nice to you usually are so because they want something.

19. If you can't be with the one you love, honey, love the one you're with.

20. If you've got it, don't flaunt it.

21. People look for evidence to support an opinion they have already got, and they can usually find it (so don't just assume what someone is saying is true).

22. If you are in a secret relationship, you probably shouldn't be in it.

23. You have to keep up with change.

24. Live so that when your children think of fairness, caring and integrity they think of you.

25. If you're going to make a change, you need to start with the man in the mirror.

26. If things seem to be too good to be true, they usually *are* too good to be true.

27. Fix your roof when the sun is shining.

28. Don't make things serious that don't have to be.

29. Don't bet more than you can afford to lose – especially on a game where you don't know all the rules.

30. We don't want someone we agree with all the time, but we do want someone we trust all the time.

31. Power corrupts; absolute power corrupts absolutely.

32. If you're not part of the steamroller, you're just part of the road.

33. Life's too short not to smell the flowers along the way.

34. Live and let live but don't live with injustice.

35. Nil illegitimi carborundum.

36. Just because someone's not on the same path as you, doesn't mean they're lost.

37. Don't let a little dispute ruin a great friendship.

38. Be careful what you wish for.

39. It's not enough to be honest; people have to believe that you're honest.

40. When you have a dispute, get out of the office, sit down, have a cup of tea and chat directly.

41. The bigger the decision, the more important it is to sleep on it.

42. If you are always honest you don't have to remember anything.

43. If a child lives with security he learns to have faith in himself and those about him.

44. There is a quick, easy, ready-made solution to every problem. Unfortunately it's usually the wrong solution.

45. Tackle head on the 'elephant in the room' and turn it to your advantage.

46. Finish off your opponents when you're in a position to do so.

47. Ageing is an unavoidable truth – you just do the best with what you've got.

48. The things that really count in your life can't be counted.

49. The price you have to pay for making a choice is wondering what would have happened if you had made a different decision.

50. If you don't decide what is worth doing, someone else will decide for you.

Postscript

I am particularly grateful to my good friend of 30 years or so, Chris Norman, who served as my devil's advocate whilst writing this book and pointed out to me many shortcomings, errors and 'opportunities for improvement' when it was at first draft stage. He did it in a well-meaning and kindly manner and the book is the better for his input. He also encouraged me to write a letter to my grandchildren's grandchildren. It's something we should all do as maybe – one day – they'll be interested. So I've included that as the last thing in the book.

I am also indebted to Ian McNeill who not only proofread the book but was my guide on many historical events.

So why seven Golden Rules for a happy life?

It's not a coincidence that there are seven wonders of the world and only seven days in a week. Any more and we'd lose track. The same goes for deadly sins. There are seven colours in a rainbow, seven ages of man, seven dwarves with Snow White and so on. The number seven is pretty special. It's the most that the neuroscientists tell us we can remember in our short-term memory. Seven is the max.

For psychologists, short-term memory refers to things that are being used by your brain right now. For example, the words you read in this book were being stored in your short-term memory and, by and large, were only there for a short period of time. Nothing to do with me, you understand, it would be the same if you were reading someone who could really write. Hopefully, your brain has extracted some meaning from these words and then the meaning is either stored or discarded. You may have some memory of some of the rules and lessons by tomorrow but most of the actual words will be lost.

Chris Norman also challenged me as to what the book WAS. What was its purpose? And I distilled it down in that it should be – first and foremost – an enjoyable read.

He and I are members of the same book club. Peter, Stephen, Rob, Chris and I read an eclectic mix of books from classics to autobiographies of northern comediennes (the lowest score ever if you recall), from psychological thrillers to war memoirs. And each month we meet and score the book we've read out of ten on two criteria – firstly was it 'engaging'? Was it a page turner? Was it a pleasure to pick it up each time? And secondly, was it thought-provoking? Did it make us think? Each book therefore has a score out of 20.

And so I wrote this book as an enjoyable read but also so that it has you thinking about life, happiness, success and fulfilment.

It has lessons for life and I used the Tudor period as a conduit to make the points. Don't worry if you don't remember the dates – you can just Google them. The key thing for me is that you take away the seven Golden Rules and the other 50 lessons we should all learn from the reigns of Henry VIII and his three children.

Letter to my grandchildren's grandchildren

Unfortunately I only really knew one grandparent – my father's father, Harry Hesketh. His youngest son – Billy – had been killed in an aeroplane accident eight months before I was born and my grandad laughed very little for the rest of his life. My father's mother – Annie Hesketh – died when I was just four so I have little or no memory of her. My mother's father died when my mother was only one year old and her mother died when she was 15 so she was effectively orphaned and tossed from aunt to aunt until she married my father. Quite frankly it's all very sad and I hope you have better luck.

My paternal great-great grandfather was Robert Hesketh. He was born in 1810 in Wigan and married Rebecca Brown in 1829. He was a greengrocer and lived on King Street in Dukinfield. He died in November 1861 in Ashton Infirmary with his son, John, by his side. He was only 51. And that's pretty much all I know about him, other than he made a will – a rare event in those days – and there's documentary evidence that the will was 'proven' in February 1862. The will talks of him owning eight 'dwelling houses' so I guess he had a bit of money but, if he did, I've no idea what happened to it. I'd love to know more about him – how he met Rebecca and what his values were. How he lived, loved and laughed. I would love to read a letter from him to me right now but that's not going to happen.

But what I can do is write a letter to you, so here it is...

* * *

Dear Great-great grandchild

Way back in 2012, a palliative care nurse, Bronnie Ware, wrote a book about the top five regrets of the dying. In it she said the biggest regret of people when they knew they were shuffling off this mortal coil was that they hadn't had the courage to live their life true to themselves; that they felt they had lived the life others *expected* of them. When people realise that their life is almost over and look back clearly on it, it is easy to see how many dreams have gone unfulfilled.

And that is true of me too.

'I could have' and 'I should have' are the biggest frustrations. Maybe I would never have been a top-class runner but I'd like to have had the opportunities to find out. And I think my parents could have – and should have – encouraged me more as I showed promise as a runner. I should have passed my 11+ (an exam taken at 10 years old that determined what school you went to from 11 years old – a ridiculous idea looking back) and I regret my parents didn't know enough about it to have tutored me and explained how important it was.

But there again, my childhood wasn't my fault.

They loved me and I was surrounded by aunts and uncles who showered me with love and helped me become confident. For reasons that went to the grave with them, quite a number of those aunts and uncles had no children of their own so I was spoilt a little. I had also arrived just eight months after Uncle Billy had been so tragically killed at the age of just 20 and I was conscious throughout my childhood that I was a bitter-sweet reminder of him.

I was taught tolerance and learned to be patient, I was taught to share and learned to be generous, I was taught 'right from wrong' and have endeavoured to live my life with the values of fairness and honesty. With your great-great grandmother we taught our darling boys, David, Daniel and Sebastian, to have good values.

I met her at a dance.

Believe it or not there were no mobile phones then (or whatever you call your device now) and I was pretty much dragged out one dark, wintery January night in Newcastle, where I was studying psychology, by one of my university friends and flatmates, Christopher 'Walt' Leech. I'm very proud of the fact that the five guys I lived with at university are still meeting for our reunion now we are well into our sixties.

Walt suggested we should strike up a conversation with two young ladies. One of them was your great-great grandmother. It's the best thing I ever did.

We married 18 months later and constantly worked to make a better life for our children. The happiness was in the journey.

When I was 50 I left the world of advertising to become a professional speaker. The real drive was that we wanted to change the weather in February. And we did! Or rather, we changed it for us by buying a plane ticket, spending February and March in the Antipodes for the next 17 years – and me entertaining audiences in sunny Australia and New Zealand.

We had a ball.

I hope you have one, too.

Here are my thoughts for you.

DECIDE ON YOUR OWN PRIORITIES

Your top three priorities should be family, career and friendships. And your career is a priority mainly so you can look after your family. After that you can only achieve so much. Don't do sport if it doesn't float your boat. Do so if it does.

I happen to like doing things I'm not very good at. Golf, running, skiing and tennis are all activities I spend plenty of time doing in the last third of my life but I accept I'll never be very good at them. But that's not the point. They're just games. It's just recreation. And if participating in these games means I get to spend time with my friends – and, for most of those activities, some of my family too – I'm happy. I see sport as a conduit to spend time with people I like. The games are a means to an end.

So spend your time on activities you choose rather than allow someone else to choose for you. Just follow your arrow wherever it points.

Some years ago I wrote my own Desiderata for my grand-children's children. The original Desiderata was written by Max Ehrmann in the 1920s and had sound wisdom within it such as 'if you compare yourself with others, you may become vain and bitter'.

So I wrote my own version of that with more practical advice such as 'don't buy cheap bin liners' and 'don't eat sprouts unless there's someone standing over you'.

Now when you come to read this – my guess is around 2100 – you'll probably not have bin liners and sprouts will no longer be available (they were rather weird-tasting vegetables that were supposedly good for you) so I am dispensing what might only very loosely be called 'advice' to you based on love, relationships and ambition that I think will last the test of time. The only thing that is truly reliable is that I loved your grandparents, Amelia, Lottie and Lily (and the others that were just a glint in your great-grandfathers' eyes when I wrote this), and that what

I am writing to you is not based on fact but rather my own meandering experiences though life.

AIM TO LEAVE EVERYTHING A LITTLE BETTER THAN YOU FOUND IT

A lot was accomplished before you were born and although I hope you will make a meaningful, positive contribution in your life and the lives of the people around you, you should be modest about what you do and achieve. Be courageous and step outside your comfort zone. But not all the time. It's called a comfort zone because it's comfortable in there. Fact is, when you look back on life you are much more likely to regret the things you didn't do rather then the things you did. We all leave the odd stain on life's carpet but if you just aim to develop loving relationships, be fair with people in everything you do and help others to achieve their dreams, you will leave everything a little better than you found it.

DON'T WORRY IF YOU CAN'T GIVE YOUR OWN CHILDREN THE BEST OF EVERYTHING

Just ensure you give them *your* best. Every day. Shower them with love but don't allow them to misbehave. That's what my wife and I did for our three wonderful sons.

Don't buy things you don't need with money you haven't got to impress people you don't like. Experiences and memories are worth more than any 'thing' you can buy. And what really matters in life is your reputation. So always keep your promises, do what you say you are going to do and be *careful* when you make promises. You can't do it all and you can't achieve it all. And you certainly can't have it all.

After all, where would you put it?

I'm only sorry I won't be able to see you grow and develop. But these three tips I give you with all my heart.

- Decide on your own priorities.

- Aim to leave everything a little better than you found it.

- Don't worry if you can't give your own children the best of everything.

Good luck.

About the author

Philip Hesketh is a full-time professional speaker.

Celebrated the world over for his ability to entertain and inspire, he reveals powerful, life-changing techniques to persuade, influence and succeed in the workplace and in our personal lives. A successful businessman, best-selling author, and one of the world's most sought-after speakers, he has inspired audiences and clients in over 20 countries to increase sales, establish value to hold higher prices and control conversations building stronger relationships. Unique for his *real-world takeaways*, he is the author of two other books, *How to Persuade and Influence People* and *Persuade.*

For more details and a video of Philip speaking, visit: www.heskethtalking.com